Belton,
A once rural, 'marke

Copyright © 2020 Ken
Cover design by Kenr.
Book design by Kenneth John Botwright

For permission requests, contact the publisher.
Published by Kenneth John Botwright
26 Orwell Crescent, Belton, Great Yarmouth NR31 9NZ
Kenbotwrightkenb08@outlook.com

Printed in Great Britain by
Book Printing Online (Part of AnchorPrint Group Ltd)
11 Victoria Street,
Syston,
Leicestershire
LE7 2LE

ISBN 978-1-8380838-0-9

Preface

My grandfather kept a diary during the interwar years, mainly about his daily tasks on the Market Garden. It occurred to me that this was a fragment of social history in a Suffolk village that many people may know nothing about. The content of this book is a combination of the diary contents, local history and the social and technological change that he witnessed during his lifetime, 1891 to 1972. I hope that you find this interesting, entertaining, will smile a lot, think about times gone by and occasionally say 'well I never knew that'.

With acknowledgement to, and in memory of, family members no longer with us.

With sincere and grateful acknowledgment to Jane Applegate, Tony Beare, Carol Goreham, Jenny Hilling, Peter Searby and others who may have unwittingly contributed, whose range of local historical knowledge proved instrumental in the compilation of this book.

The majority of the images used are the property of the author or have been provided, with their consent, by friends. Those sourced, are either in the public domain or have a Creative Commons License with appropriate attribution.

Contents

Introduction 4

  The Family 9

  Frud's children 16

The Family Name 21

Harriet the Laundress 24

1891 to 1905 the early years 31

Trades, shops and pubs 43

1905 to 1914 pre war 49

World War One 57

  Frud's Navy Service 61

1918 to 1939 the interwar years 72

Frud's Diaries 93

  Staff 93

  Farming and Market Gardening 98

  Harvesting and Packing 115

  Mechanisation 120

  Non Farming activities 125

  Out and About 126

    Buying 126

    Auctions 129

    Deliveries 132

Entertainment 133

    At Home 147

    Some of Frud's Diary entries, in his own words! 149

World War Two 155

    Frud's diary entries during WW2, in his own words!...... 158

    Peter's Navy Service 169

    The Thornborough, Normandy Landings and beyond . 172

    Fire on board the SS Empire Patrol. 177

    Planned resistance: Auxiliary Units. 182

1945 to 1952 Dissolution 186

1952 to 1964 Hornerthorpe 194

1965 to 1972 Roman Way 207

Lothingland 219

    Places of Interest in Lothingland 222

    Gariannonum, the Roman Fort at Burgh Castle 236

Belton 238

Introduction

This book is based around Frud (1891-1972) and his diary, recording life on a market garden in a rural Suffolk village. It conveys social and local history, humorous anecdotes, technological change and life during two world wars.

Fred, colloquially known as Frud, and by his wife Anne (pronounced by Fred as Annie) as Freddums, lived through a time of massive change including the mechanisation of the agricultural and horticultural industry with internal combustion engine–powered tractors replacing steam and horse power.

Frud was a young boy at the time of the Battle of Omdurman and the Boer War, he also lived through two world wars, serving in the Royal Navy in the First World War. He experienced the demise of the pony and trap as the main method of transportation, and horses which were the main form of power and haulage, gradually being replaced by the internal combustion engine–powered motor cars, vans and lorries.

The rail network and the steam railway locomotive was well established by the time Frud was born and indeed provided the catalyst for the establishment and expansion of numerous market gardens in the village of Belton. Produce could be shipped from Belton and Burgh railway station anywhere in the country for sale the next day. This provided a further outlet for the market gardens, as, up until the arrival of the railway, the market for their produce was literally the centuries-old market at Great Yarmouth, local shops and hostelries. As late as the 1960s, three quarters of the stalls on great Yarmouth market were occupied by market gardeners, travelling from up to 10 miles away to sell their produce. The arrival of the railway in the 19th century stimulated the growth of market gardens by providing quick access to the major urban markets. The family market garden produced and shipped tomatoes, cucumbers, rhubarb and cut flowers to Newcastle, Birmingham, Glasgow, Leeds and London. The railway arrived in Belton in 1859 and closed in 1959, a period which exactly coincided with the expansion, heyday and subsequent demise of the market garden in Belton.

Belton & Burgh Station, goods and coal yard
With kind permission of Dick Lindsay – Belton/Burgh Castle Mardle, Norfolk

Boxes of flowers being loaded on to the train,
circa 1930s
With kind permission of Dick Lindsay – Belton/Burgh Castle Mardle, Norfolk

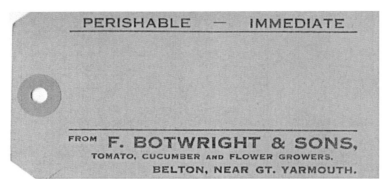

Every box had a delivery label

Steam train passing through/leaving Belton &
Burgh Station

With kind permission of Dick Lindsay – Belton/Burgh Castle Mardle, Norfolk

Waiting for the train to pass.
With kind permission of Dick Lindsay – Belton/Burgh Castle Mardle, Norfolk

Although the railway was advantageous to the market garden industry, it also had its disadvantages, as the sparks from the coal fired steam engines frequently ignited the heather and gorse as it wound its way across Belton Common, an example of this appeared in the Yarmouth Independent in the early 1900s.

Heath Fire, a fire near the railway line on Belton Common, near Yarmouth, gave people living in Henry Terrace close by an anxious two hours before its progress was broken. Between four and six acres of heather and gorse were burnt.

Police constable Button, of Belton, and Mobile-officers Snell and Todd, of Lowestoft, could do little to arrest the fire at first. When it began to threaten the houses they, with other helpers, cut away the gorse and tried to smother the flames with soil. The flames spread under two electricity pylons and fused a cable, causing an explosion. Police-constable Button, however, had already telephoned for the current to be cut off, and after the fire the supply was unaffected. London and North Eastern Railway (LNER) employees, under the supervision of the relief stationmaster, and other parishioners helped the police.

The Family

The Botwrights hadn't always lived in Belton, Frud's grandfather Emmanuel came from Lound, his father John being a thatcher. Working class people were generally reliant on walking as their means of getting about and consequently sought a wife from within their village, so everybody was related to everybody else. In the late 19th century there may have been an informal Government directive, directing the young males of English villages to travel further afield i.e. to neighbouring villages to seek a wife, to prevent inbreeding and the subsequent, so called at the time, 'village idiot'. Eugenics was a relatively new 'life science' but people were probably becoming aware of the folly and likely outcome of inbreeding.

Emmanuel had a child with Harriet Lawn, listed in the census as Emmanuel Lawn, as they say in Suffolk 'putting the cart before the horse' he then married Harriet and had a further three sons George, John and Fred senior (Frud's father). George died aged 8 and John moved to North Shields, leaving Fred senior to run the market garden of which he made a great success. Emmanuel Lawn married Emily Reeve whose family owned a farm in Bradwell, he later changed his name to Emmanuel Botwright.

Frud's Grandfather, Emmanuel Botwright
1828-1896

Fred snr left with his brother John, circa 1890

Fred senior married Lucy Marchant Bottoms in 1892 and had seven children: Frud, Harriet (aka

Joy), John, Margaret (aka Maggie), Roger, Harry and Lucy. With the exception of John, who drowned aged two in one of the open water tanks that fed the glass house heating pipes, all of Fred senior's children and their spouses worked on the market garden and farm. The business also employed several villagers. Agricultural and horticultural work was still very labour intensive at this time and the main means of employment in a rural village.

L to R Emmanuel, Frud, Lucy, Maggie, Fred Snr, Joy and Harriet, circa 1905
Frud, Joy and Maggie's parents, Fred and Lucy, and grandparents Emmanuel and Harriet.

L to R - Joy, Grandmother Harriet, Maggie and Frud, circa 1903

L to R Frud, Joy, Maggie, Lucy and Roger, circa 1908

Harriet's husband Emmanuel, despite becoming a property owner through marriage, appeared to 'jog along' with the land, indeed rumour has it that he was often absent, and, combined with his appearance, tantamount to a vagrant. Harriet and her son Fred senior, doubtless fed up with Emmanuel's frequent absences and lackadaisical approach to work, were not that enamoured with him and sadly he ended his days, together with his brother Frank in the dreaded workhouse at Oulton. Once Fred senior was of age the potential of the site was exploited. This mainly came in the form of glasshouses, enabling the growing season to be extended and more delicate and lucrative produce to be grown e.g. tomatoes, cucumbers and tender cut flowers.

Frud's children

Frud had three children during the period between the first and second world wars Marjorie born in 1920, Peter born in 1922 and Derek born in 1932. Derek was probably conceived in error as he arrived ten years after Frud and Anne's last child Peter. Frud had a habit of lifting the lid of an old wooden chest with his toe as he lay on the chaise longue after a hard day's work, fiddling with it, as they say in Suffolk. This however stopped when young Derek suddenly jumped on said chest when Frud's toe was under the lid. Derek learnt a lot of new words that day! Peter, aged 10, attending a friend's birthday party was asked what games he wanted to play, he looked at his friend with disdain and stated *"I h'e n't come here to play games, I've come here to eat."*

Belton school photo, Class II of 1933, Peter is on the back row third from the left.

In summer, Frud's daughter would sell posies of flowers to holiday makers on day trips from Great Yarmouth to Belton Gardens. The younger village children would run after the charabanc as it was leaving, collecting pennies that were thrown to them by the visitors. The Kings Head also held carnivals at this time.

Belton Gardens, Kings Head - Brakes and Charabancs, circa 1920s

Belton Kings Head with Brakes and Coaches, circa 1930s

With kind permission of Dick Lindsay – Belton/Burgh Castle Mardle, Norfolk

Belton Gardens, Kings Head, circa 1920s

Horse drawn Shooting Brakes (historically used for shooting parties) and Charabancs were open top wagons with seats. Open top motorised 'charabancs' and 'brakes' developed in the early part of the 20th century, having rows of bench seats looking forward, commonly used for large parties as public conveyances for excursions. The holiday makers arrived at the Kings Head in both horse drawn and motorised brakes and charabancs. Some charabancs had a large canvas folding hood stowed at the rear in case of rain.

Charabanc

Harold F.B. Wheeler (https://commons.wikimedia.org/wiki/File:Charabanc.jpg), „Charabanc", marked as public domain, more details on Wikimedia Commons: https://commons.wikimedia.org/wiki/Template:PD-old

Frud wasn't particularly domesticated, during the periods when Anne was unwell or away he couldn't be doing with cooking for himself or setting the table, he simply took a chair into the walk-in pantry and sat there helping himself to the food within, this also alleviated washing up! Similarly, his cooking prowess was lacking when required to provide food for Anne. The usual option was to cook sausages in a frying pan, normally burnt to a crisp, delivered to Anne in said greasy frying pan. This annoyed her immensely with the grease from the pan daubed all over the clean white sheets and this was accompanied by a whole loaf of bread, not even cut into slices. Whenever Anne broke something, like a cup, Frud would irritatingly yet risibly say "Whatever did you do that for?" as if she had done it on purpose.

Frud's daughter, Marjorie married Bertie Saul in 1943. She was quite naïve having lead a sheltered life. On their wedding night, with Bertie preparing to consummate the marriage, Marjorie, simply screamed and hid in the wardrobe. She must have eventually surfaced though, her son Tony was born in February 1945!

The Family Name

The family name of Botwright was possibly derived from Boatwright, builder of boats, and indeed on some censuses was spelt this way. The name is derived from the Old English word "bat" meaning boat, and "wyrhta" meaning wright, and thus, would have been a boat builder or ship's carpenter. There is also supposition that this was the name of the man who helped build William the Conquerors fleet that invaded

England in 1066. Bayeux, near Caen in France, was the launching point for the Norman Conquest. There is an ancient ruined fortress on the coast near Caen called "La forteresse de Batuvrai" (Boatright). Some of the residents in the area said that it was the keep (fortified tower) of the royal shipwright to William himself. In the Doomsday Book, there is mentioned lands given to William's most faithful vassals and servants, among them a shipwright ("Batuvrai"). The Normans were descended from Vikings who were given feudal lordship of areas in the Duchy of Normandy in the 10th century. The Bot/Boatwrights in the USA have confirmed their Viking ancestry through DNA testing.

From 1435 to 1474, John Botwright was rector of St. Peter and St. Paul Swaffham. Among the monuments in this church is an altar-tomb, with the effigy of John Botwright, D.D. (Doctor of Divinity) who was Master of Corpus Christi College, Cambridge, chaplain to Henry VI., and vicar of this church. John was unanimously chosen as Master of Corpus Christi College, University of Cambridge in 1443, during the Feast of St. Mark the Evangelist, having been a "proctor" with the Master John Wolpit. John was awarded a coat-of-arms in 1443 by King Henry VI when he was made Master of Corpus Christi College, in which capacity he served until his death in 1474. John was made Chaplain to King Henry VI in 1447.

Coat-of-Arms granted to John Botewright, D.D.
(Master of the College of Corpus Christi)
With grateful acknowledgement to http://www.boatwrightgenealogy.com/

23

Another John Botwright is recorded as living in the County of Suffolk in 1469. In 1524 one John Botewrighte is listed in the "Subsidy Rolls" of Suffolk. Botwrights have been traced back to the 16th century in north central Suffolk and genealogy shows their passage through time from there via Botesdale, Hoxne, Bungay, Thwaite, Denton, Stockton, Mutford, Wangford, Lowestoft, Blundeston, Hopton and Lound to Belton and Gorleston/Yarmouth.

Harriet the Laundress

Harriet, Frud's grandmother, was the daughter of James and Mariah Lawn who also had sons John, Joseph and George and a daughter Caroline. Harriet was born in 1834 and died in 1916 when her eldest son Frud was away in the navy during WW1. From the 1851 census it appears that Harriet had an illegitimate daughter named as Harriet Reynolds.

Harriet Lawn was listed in the census as a laundress, a woman who 'took in' washing. In the 19th century it was very rare for a woman to go out to work, women at this time were usually fully occupied in the home, there were no 'mod cons' such as vacuum cleaners, washing machines or cookers. Housework, cooking, cleaning, washing and looking after the sizeable families, 12 children was not unheard of, took up most of the time. Harriet would not therefore have been able to go out to work, but, as in this case, she could have work brought to her as in washing for other villagers. With no washing machines this was hard work and those who could afford it would send their washing to a laundress.

The Census of 1851 stated that Belton had seven laundresses, including one in Browston. By 1861 laundresses had increased to twenty four. Taking in laundry continued in the 1920's and 30's, with boarding house owners in Great Yarmouth being availed of this service.

Washing was undertaken in an outside 'wash house or outhouse' usually attached to the main house or close by. Washing was a manual, 'hands-on' process, first the laundress had to light a fire under the 'copper' a large deep cauldron with a wooden lid, in a brick built frame with a space underneath for the fire.

A coal fired copper built into a brickwork furnace, usually located in a 'wash house'. Standing beside the furnace is a wooden dolly drum and a dolly stick on top.

Water was heated in the 'copper', this could then be used to boil the laundry adding soap grated from a bar. Washing was lifted out of the copper with a stick. The hot water was also transferred to a wooden dolly tub where a dolly stick with short wooden legs would be used to agitate (pound and stir) the washing.

A wooden washing dolly stick used in a wooden dolly tub.

At this point a washboard and a bar of laundry soap may also be used for stubborn stains. During the rinsing of the laundry, 'laundry blue' would be added for whitening bed sheets and shirts, the most common of these being Reckitt's blue bags.

The washing was then wrung in a mangle to squeeze the water out of the laundry before hanging it outside on a 'linen line' to dry and then it would be hung on a 'clothes horse' to 'air' (remove any damp that remained). A mangle was two wooden rollers in a huge cast iron frame which had to be operated by hand. The washing was placed between the rollers and the handle cranked which squeezed the water out and pulled it through the rollers. If you had heavy thick material you could adjust the rollers' gap, it may have taken 2 or 3 goes to get the water out during which time the gap could be reduced. The effort required to turn the crank handle was enormous and most laundresses developed large arm muscles as a result of this work.

A mangle, colloquially known as a wringer.
David M Jones

Most people at this time had a daily stand-up wash at the kitchen sink i.e. face, neck, arms and pits, as bathing was such a laborious and time consuming task. Bathing involved getting the tin bath indoors, heating enough water in the coal fired copper, and bucketing it into the bath. This task was therefore usually undertaken just once a week. All the family would bath in turn i.e. when one got out another got in, in the same bath water! A tin bath was still used by many families well into the 1960s.

1891 to 1905 the early years

Frud was born on the 20th September 1891 at Jesse Terrace, Burgh Castle; his mother Lucy's family home. He lived at Pansy Villa in Belton, located on the market garden, from 1891, initially with his father Fred, mother Lucy, brothers and sisters and from 1919 with his wife Anne and later with their children Marjorie (1920), Peter (1922) and Derek (1932) until 1952. Frud's father Fred, bought the adjacent Beech Farm, Belton in 1919 and lived there whilst Frud and Anne remained at Pansy Villa.

Pansy Villa, Beccles Road, Belton

Pansy Villa was located on Lawn's Lane off Beccles Road, Belton, possibly built by Fred Snr in the late 19th century. This locale may therefore have been where the Lawn family had lived for some time, in a small cottage further up the lane, since demolished. Early maps show a small parcel of land of about 4 acres surrounding Pansy Villa, from which at the time, a living could be made. Beccles Road was previously called Belton Hall Road and Belton Green Road. The latter due to the fact that the road lead to the once sizeable medieval Village Green, since lost to houses. Many authors over the past 200 years have written of the Green and it is generally believed to be the location of the origin and main settlement of Belton. This is the location of the highest concentration of 17th/18th century listed buildings within the village i.e. Belton Old Hall, Beech Farm Tithe Barn, and the Thatched Cottage. It has been surmised that the Beech Farm farmhouse, Belton (House) Lodge, Belton Hall and the White House on Church Lane, and numerous old houses on Station Road South have much older 17th century foundations.

An approximation of the Village Green

'Reproduced with the permission of the National Library of Scotland (CC BY 4.0)'

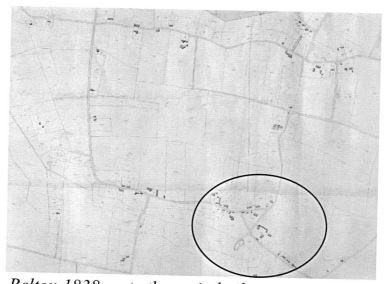

Belton 1838, note the main built-up area around the plausible location of the Village Green

Pansy Villa was a reasonable house for the time, having two front sitting rooms, a living room, a walk-in pantry with shelving, four bedrooms, a glazed, covered way with concrete floor, attached lean-to kitchen, lean-to conservatory, pump of drinking water and a brick and tiled earth closet (outside privy / toilet). Emulsion paint wasn't commercially available until the 1950s and the installation of wallpaper was expensive and time consuming, the walls in the house were therefore whitewashed. Whitewash or lime paint is a low-cost type of paint made from slaked lime, chalk and water. It is traditionally used for interiors in food preparation areas, particularly rural dairies, specifically due to its mildly antibacterial properties.

Traditionally, "market garden" was used to contrast farms devoted to raising vegetables and berries, a specialized type of farming, with the larger branches of grain, dairy, and orchard fruit farming; agricultural historians continue to thus use the term. Such operations were not necessarily small-scale. Indeed, many were very large, commercial farms that were called "gardens" not because of size, but because English-speaking farmers traditionally referred to their vegetable plots as "gardens": in English whether in common parlance or in anthropological or historical scholarship, husbandry done by the hoe is customarily called "gardening" and husbandry done by the plough as "farming" regardless of the scale of either.

Frud went to Belton School, there were no primary, middle or secondary schools at this time, children went to the one village school from age 5 to 12. The Census of 1851 stated that out of 158 children in Belton of 12 years and under, only 14 are recorded as scholars, school was obviously not well attended. Children from poor families were kept away to do jobs like bird scaring, stone picking and helping with the harvest. Education was not free, nor was it compulsory at this time. Many children worked outside school hours, in 1901 the national figure was put at 300,000, and truancy was a major problem due to the fact that parents could not afford to give up income earned by their children. Prior to an 1880 Act, making education compulsory, school attendance was

very haphazard as rural children worked on the
land instead of going to school.

*Four children in the photo helping with the
harvest*
With kind permission of Dick Lindsay – Belton/Burgh Castle Mardle, Norfolk

*Belton School group photo with Sir John Mills'
father, Lewis Mills (head teacher) back left.*

Frud wasn't that sporty but he had his moments. Whilst playing football one day, the exertion of kicking the ball caused Frud to fart rather loudly, resulting in the goal keeper collapsing in a heap helpless with laughter, and enabling Frud to, somewhat fortuitously, score a goal!

Pansy Villa had an open pit for the waste water from the washing of the residents, their clothes, dishes and cooking pots and pans. Frud as a young inquisitive child usually ended up falling in the dirty water pit and being hosed down outside by his mother. There were no flush toilets at this time and the sewage system was not installed in the village until 1964.

Frud, even at school, was not averse to playing an occasional prank on someone, including the teachers. The toilets at the village school were outside with a bucket, shaped like a fireman's helmet, under a wooden bench with a hole in it through which a deposit was made into the aforesaid bucket. This bucket when full had to be emptied and this was accessed from the back. This was where one of his pranks was undertaken, a bunch of stinging nettles was gathered on the way to school and placed upright like a bunch of flowers in the bucket so the next teacher to use the toilet got his or her backside stung.

Wooden toilets, with bucket underneath and accessed, when needing emptying, from the back.

DeFacto (https://commons.wikimedia.org/wiki/File:Townsend_House_privy_-
_the_inside.jpg), https://creativecommons.org/licenses/by-sa/4.0/legalcode

Another transgression involved the Teacher's prize marrow, Frud decided to stand on the marrow to see if it could stand his weight, it didn't, and needless to say it squashed, he then buried it to hide the evidence.

During Frud's early years his father was
establishing the business of growing under glass
i.e. horticulture in glasshouses, extending the
growing season. Fred senior's father in law,
Henry Bottom, was head gardener at a large
estate in Norfolk, possibly Blickling Hall as he
lived at both Banningham and Burgh next
Aylsham, he introduced Fred to, what was then
considered as, exotic fruit and vegetables. He
taught Fred senior how to grow tomatoes and
cucumbers under glass, the need for sterilisation
and fumigation of the soil, pots and glasshouses,
how to trim non-fruit producing shoots,
trimming their leaves, a continuous and time
consuming task, staking, wiring and stringing
tomato and cucumber plants, how to make a
cucumber bed with furrough/gorse bushes,
leaves and soil, and how to hand-pollinate
cucumbers, being indoors there is less likelihood
of this task being undertaken by natural
pollinators. A feather was used to transfer the
yellow pollen from the male anther onto the
stigma in the centre of the female flower a
tedious and painstaking process. Another
regular task was the carting by tumbrel of fresh,
uncontaminated soil which was then took into

the glasshouses by wheelbarrow, a back breaking task. As should by now be obvious, the growing of cucumbers and tomatoes was an extremely labour intensive task, e.g. it took one man all day just to irrigate. Early rhubarb and chrysanthemums for the Christmas market were also grown under glass, being 'out of season' a premium price could be achieved and this was indeed very lucrative.

Fires in the glasshouses and the subsequent smoke, appear to have been undertaken 3 or 4 times per week to keep the pests away, it wasn't until the middle of the 20th century that synthetic insecticides and pesticides were widely used. From the 17th century to the mid-20th century nicotine and arsenic were used! The 19th century saw the introduction of two more natural pesticides, pyrethrum, which is derived from chrysanthemums, and rotenone, which is derived from the roots of tropical vegetables. Whitewash made from slaked lime and chalk was painted on the inside of the glass before the crops were established to reduce the heat within the greenhouse, otherwise in the summer the plants would have cooked.

Henry Bottom

All of the large estates of the landed gentry had a heated glass house to enable the growing and provision of fruit such as grapes, oranges, peaches and pineapples for most of the year to impress their guests. This also provided cut flowers throughout the winter months, enabling the provision of cut flowers for the house all year round. It was this little known knowledge that Lucy's father Henry imparted to Fred senior, introducing him to, what was at this time, a new business venture.

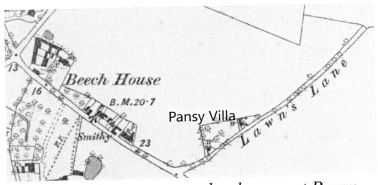

In 1884 there were no glasshouses at Pansy Villa, this would soon change under Henry's direction.

Trades, shops and pubs

The population of Belton when Frud was born in 1891 was 752. There were many trades practiced in Belton at this time including: blacksmith, wheelwright, coffin maker, carpenter, joiner, shoe / bootmaker, builder, bricklayer, coal / coke merchant, and threshing machine proprietor.

The Blacksmith was crucial to the local market gardeners and farmers, not only did they shoe horses and fit iron tyres to cart wheels, they were also indispensable for the repair of horticultural implements, making gates, hinges and general iron work for wagons etc.

The Blacksmith's Shop (Smithy) at Beccles Road, Belton

The Blacksmiths, with iron tyre in foreground

Despite being a relatively small village, there were numerous shops in Belton during Frud's lifetime including: 2 pork shops, 2 confectionary / tobacconist shops, 2 bicycle repair shops, 7 general stores / grocery shops, a butchers, a bakers, 2 boot / shoe repairers and 2 wet fish shops.

In Belton and Browston in the mid-19th century there were 3 market gardeners, by the turn of the 19th / 20th century, after the arrival of the railway in the village of Belton, there were 31 market gardeners. The railway opening up significant new markets for the produce. Half of these were large market gardens with a significant acreage and a substantial area under glass but many were making a living on a small parcel of land.

Grocers, butchers and bakers delivered their produce at this time, if Anne was cutting flowers up the field, she wrote her order in chalk on the outside of the house door e.g. "4 large breasts (chicken) and a crusty bloomer".

There were four pubs or 'Ale / Beer Houses' in Belton, the Kings Head, the Railway Tavern, the Dove, on Beccles Road and the Gull on The Green. A beerhouse was a type of drinking establishment created in the United Kingdom by the 1830 Beerhouse Act, legally defined as a place "where beer is sold to be consumed on the premises". Public houses at the time were issued with licences by local magistrates under the terms of the Retail Brewers Act 1828, and were subject to police inspections at any time of the day or night. The proprietors of beerhouses on the other hand simply had to buy a licence from the government costing two guineas per annum.

Belton Kings Head, with railway bridge to the right, over St Johns Road, circa 1920s

The thatched Railway Tavern

The Railway Tavern Tea Gardens, Belton.   Proprietor, W. E. Ives.

With kind permission of Dick Lindsay – Belton/Burgh Castle Mardle, Norfolk

Ted & Jean Searby leaving the Railway Tavern after WW2, drawn by Ted Searby. Ted was in the Royal Marines seeing action in the Far East and Jean was in the Auxiliary Territorial Service (ATS) the women's branch of the British Army during the Second World War.

Courtesy of Mr Peter Searby

48

1905 to 1914 pre war

Young Frud, even as a child, was expected to work on the market garden, although this was undertaken somewhat unenthusiastically. Frequently, his mother Lucy would call up the stairs, where Frud was still in bed, to inform her eldest son that his father had then entered the house, at which point Frud would leap out of bed, hurriedly dress and exit out of the bedroom window onto the lean-to roof, fearing a severe scolding from his father for not being at work.

Frud, ever artful, disliked loading the cart with produce for market or flowers for the train station. Just as this task was imminent, Frud would say to his father, I need to go to the toilet, alright said Fred, but he soon cottoned on to this ruse to get out of loading the cart as this occurred with increasing regularity. The next time Frud said I need to go to the toilet, Fred said "No, shit your bloody self".

Yarmouth Market, circa 1900

Frud age 16

The adult Frud's character was comedic, he relished pulling someone's leg, teasing and convincing them of something that wasn't always true; he could be cantankerous and argumentative, sometimes just for self-gratification. Frud never appeared to be embarrassed by anything and never shy, characterised by being more extrovert than introvert. He was also very crafty, cunning, artful and not unintelligent. He was adept at latently convincing or persuading someone, bringing them round to his point of view.

Anne was a jovial character, hardworking, prim and proper but could 'fly off the handle' (lose her temper) or 'put her parts on' (have an outburst) if anyone upset, angered or annoyed her. This part of her character was played on by Frud, mostly unintentionally but sometimes intentionally, he liked to rile her. He found it amusing to annoy or irritate Anne, who would flare up, but she soon calmed down. Woe betide Frud if he shew her up in public, if he did something indecorous or embarrassing. Anne would usually tut followed by 'oh for goodness sake Freddums'.

Frud began courting Anne Buck who lived at Low Road, Haddiscoe. He travelled from Belton along the Beccles Road (A143) and across the Haddiscoe Dam (a road derived from an ancient causeway) to visit Anne by pony and trap, the pony therefore new the way very well having made the journey on countless occasions. It was not unusual for Frud to have a few pints in the Haddiscoe Crown with his future brothers-in-law Tom and Kenny. The outcome of which was inevitably inebriation, no cars to talk of and no drink driving laws at this time. Tom and Kenny would load Frud into the trap, slap the horse on the rump and it would then take Frud home to Belton, the horse knew the well-trodden way only too well. If anyone saw the apparent apparition of a driverless pony and trap travelling across the misty and marshy Haddiscoe Dam late at night, they must have imagined ghostly goings on!

Anne Buck age 18

Frud's working attire included combination all-in-one vest and long john underwear, a collarless shirt, neckerchief, woollen trousers with an extremely high waistband nearly up to his chest with triangular tabs for the attachment of braces, a gansey (a hardwearing, hand knitted, woollen jumper), a cap, boots and leather gaiters to prevent the bottom of his trousers getting wet when working in the fields. Cold and wet weather required a leather wescot (waistcoat) and maybe an overcoat or oilskin. Whereas his 'Sunday best' clothes included a three piece suit, with gold watch and chain strung between the two waistcoat pockets, a shirt and detachable collar, a wide brimmed trilby and highly polished boots.

Frud didn't like it when his father told him to go ploughing due to the number of miles he had to walk a day to undertake this task. A ploughman and his horse were expected to plough an acre a day and this required both man and horse to walk 11 miles. This was hot and sweaty work and Frud experienced chafing and subsequent soreness on the insides of his buttocks. He spoke about this predicament to an old horseman who said "well boy, what you want to do is to find yourself a smooth flat stone and place it between the cheeks of your arse" and much to Frud's surprise it worked.

Frud age 24

World War One

Food production was of vital importance during World War One with the demand exceeding supply and subsequent prices increasing by 130%. Britain's farming industry was extremely labour intensive and inefficient at this time and this was exacerbated by the young men enlisting in the forces leading to a shortage of labour. Britain was also reliant on food imports from all corners of the Empire transported by sea, an avenue which the German Navy would severely disrupt.

In Britain, during the First World War, 1914 to 1918, queues for food had become dangerously long. Rationing was introduced starting with sugar in December 1917, then with meat and butter in February 1918. The ration coupons were often useless, as the supply of items just wasn't there to meet even that coupon-limited demand. This increased demand for food benefitted the market garden and farm.

Frud on the cart, making a delivery of produce to Lound Village Maid, prior to his enlisting in the Navy. Note the WW1 soldiers.

Frud did not enlist at the onset of WW1, his father would not allow it, as he was reliant on his services on the labour intensive market garden. Frud did not therefore enlist until the huge loss of life in WW1 caused the government to conscript men. Conscription during the First World War began when the British government passed the Military Service Act in 1916. The Act specified that single men aged 18 to 40 years old were liable to be called up for military service unless they were widowed with children or ministers of a religion. The law went through several changes before the war ended. Married men were exempt in the original Act, although this was changed in June 1916. It is possible that Frud's father applied to a Military Service Tribunal for exemption for his son on the grounds of damage to the business and the importance of his business to the country i.e. food supply. He may have argued that Frud was in a Reserved Occupation working in agriculture/horticulture, but the rules were unclear in this respect, unlike WW2 where coherent manpower policies, and an appropriate schedule of reserved occupations were produced ahead of the re-introduction of conscription in April 1939. The Government ordered that the records of these tribunals were to be destroyed due to their sensitive content.

British Government
(https://commons.wikimedia.org/wiki/File:Poster_Military_Service_Act_1916_Attest_
Now.jpg), „Poster Military Service Act 1916 Attest Now", marked as public domain,
more details on Wikimedia Commons:
https://commons.wikimedia.org/wiki/Template:PD-UKGov

Frud's Navy Service

Frud and Anne had been courting for some time when he received his call up papers and therefore decided to get married in October 1916. Frud's father may well have coerced him to get married as this status exempted him from military service. Such was the shortage of men, this however was subsequently changed. During World War One, Frederick Harry Botwright DA 13618 served as a Leading Deck Hand in the Royal Naval Reserve. His diary entry of the 2nd of October 1925 (7 years after the War had ended) stated "Had my medals come from the Admiralty, two Service and a Victory medal."

Frud, centre, with his two brothers-in-law Kenny Buck left and Tom Buck right.

Frud was called up and enrolled in the Navy on the 17th October 1916, at HMS Pembroke (land based Royal Naval barracks) accommodation centre, supply school, gunnery school and new entry training centre at Chatham, Kent. Prior to 1903 accommodation had been in three hulks one of which was HMS Pembroke and that name was transferred to the new barracks. Upon enrolment the following details about Frud were recorded: height 5 feet 6 ¾ inches, chest measurement 36 ½ inches, complexion fresh and blue eyes. Frud was transferred from the Royal Navy to the Royal Naval Reserve on the 9th November 1916.

Royal Naval Barracks Chatham

He left Chatham on the 10th November for Whale Island, a small island in Portsmouth Harbour close by Portsea Island and home to HMS Excellent part of the Maritime Warfare School, the oldest shore training establishment within the Royal Navy. He left there on the 18th November for HMS Vernon, a shore establishment of the Royal Navy. Vernon was established on 26th April 1876 as the Royal Navy's Torpedo Branch also known as the Torpedo School, named after the ship HMS Vernon which served as part of its floating base.

HMS Vernon

Graham Horn (https://commons.wikimedia.org/wiki/File:Former_HMS_Vernon_-_geograph.org.uk_-_808160.jpg), „Former HMS Vernon - geograph.org.uk - 808160", https://creativecommons.org/licenses/by-sa/2.0/legalcode

He left HMS Vernon for the Royal Naval Barracks Portsmouth (HMS Victory) on the 25th of November.

In the barracks, having a shower, Frud was most intrigued to see that a fellow conscript had a 'W' tattooed on each buttock, his intrigue got the better of him and he asked the chap why he had these tattoos, the chap then inadvertently, or not, dropped the soap bending over to pick it up, at which time Frud then saw the purpose of the two Ws, WOW!

Royal Naval Barracks Portsmouth (HMS Victory)

Frud, having completed his training, left HMS Victory Barracks on the 21st of January 1917 for HMS Diadem, the lead ship of the Diadem-class of protected cruiser in the Royal Navy. Frud then served on Motor Launches for the remainder of WW1 recorded in his handwritten record of his days in the Navy as follows:

Called up for the Navy on 16th of October 1916. Went to Chatham (HMS Pembroke). Left Chatham for Whale Island on the 10th of November. Left Whale Island for HMS Vernon on the 18th of November. Left HMS Vernon for Royal Naval Barracks Portsmouth (HMS Victory) on the 25th of November. Left HMS Victory Barracks on the 21st of January 1917 for HMS Diadem. Left HMS Diadem for HM Motor Launch 101 at Dover on the 4th of February. HM Motor Launch 101 was not at Dover. Left Dover on the 5th of February for HM Motor Launch 101 at Newhaven. Left HM Motor Launch 101 at Newhaven for HM Motor Launch 421 on the 18th of March. Left H M Motor Launch 421 on the 31st of

March at Newhaven for HM Motor Launch 280 at Dover. Left HM Motor Launch 280 on August 22nd for HM Motor Launch 254 at Dover. On May the 10th 1918 early-morning 254 was sunk in the Ostend raid. I joined HM Motor Launch 554, she had her stern drove in so as we had to go to Dunkirk for repairs. Left HM Motor Launch 554 at Dover for the Royal Naval Barracks Portsmouth on the 23rd of May. Left HMS Victory on the 20th of June for HM Motor Launch 225 at Swansea, South Wales. I joined it on June the 25th. Left HM Motor Launch 225 on December 12th for the Yarmouth drifter Herring Queen. Went to Milford Haven and were dismantled then came round and struck Gorleston quay two days before Christmas 1918. This finishing my life in the Navy, the place where I first went to join.

Frud's official record states that he was "dispersed to shore on demobilisation" at Great Yarmouth on January 15th 1919.

A motor launch (ML) is a small military vessel in British navy service. It was designed for harbour defence and submarine chasing or for armed high speed air-sea rescue. The first motor launches entered service in the First World War. These were 580, 80-foot-long (24m) vessels, receiving the designations ML-1 to ML-580. They served between 1916 and the end of the war with the Royal Navy defending the British coast from German submarines. Powered by two 440hp petrol engines which enabled a top speed of 19 knots. Forward was mounted a 13 pounder gun (soon replaced with a 3 pounder) and two depth charges. Additional armament consisted of lance bombs and a Lewis machine gun. The complement comprised two officers, two motor mechanics two leading seaman and four seamen.

The prime means of detecting a submarine on a motor launch was a visual sighting, but there was also a hydrophone. This was a passive listening device which could hear the engines of a submarine. To use this it was necessary for the boat to stop and lower the hydrophone over the side. By the sound received it was possible to determine the type of engine and the direction in which the vessel using the engine lay. There was no means of determining distance. Frud was a qualified hydrophone operator.

Motor Launch ML59

Domville-Fife, Charles William
(https://commons.wikimedia.org/wiki/File:Motor_Launch_ML_59.jpg), „Motor Launch ML 59", marked as public domain, more details on Wikimedia Commons: https://commons.wikimedia.org/wiki/Template:PD-1923

A sailor throwing a lance bomb, high explosive and weighing between 20 and 30lbs to be hurled (by hand) at a submarine.

Royal Navy official photographer

(https://commons.wikimedia.org/wiki/File:The_Royal_Navy_on_the_Home_Front,_1914-1918_Q18230.jpg), „The Royal Navy on the Home Front, 1914-1918 Q18230", marked as public domain, more details on Wikimedia Commons: https://commons.wikimedia.org/wiki/Template:PD-UKGov

Dazzle camouflage

Merchant vessel dazzle-painted as seen through a submarine periscope.

The same vessel on identical course painted grey.

Disorientating Dazzle

69

During WW1 a weird camouflage system was adopted. Dazzle camouflage (also known as Razzle Dazzle or Dazzle painting) was a military camouflage paint scheme used on ships, extensively during World War I and to a lesser extent in World War II. After the Allied Navies failed to develop effective means to disguise ships in all weathers, the dazzle technique was employed, not in order to conceal the ship, but rather to make it difficult for the enemy to estimate its type, size, speed and direction of travel.

THREE BELTON HEROES. Belton is proud of the fact that three of her sons-Able Seaman Frank Simpson, R.N., F. Botwright, R.N.V.R., and Private Arthur Smith, Royal Marine Artillery-took part in the recent naval successes at Zeebrugge and Ostend. Able Seaman Frank Simpson is the younger son of Mr. M. A. Simpson of 'Hope Villa', and was a member of the crew of the old cruiser Thetis, one of the old blockships which now lies at the bottom of Zeebrugge Harbour. Able Seaman Frederick Botwright, eldest son of Mr. Frederick Botwright, market gardener, was on board one of the motor launches which rendered such meritorious services both at Zeebrugge and Ostend. Although having passed through a trying ordeal, the occasion of the attack upon Ostend when his vessel was sunk, Botwright appeared quite cheerful and well when in Belton during the Whitsun holidays. Private Smith was not quite as fortunate as his two brother villagers. He was one of the party of Marines landed on the Mole at Zeebrugge from the 'Vindictive,' but had the misfortune to receive a shrapnel wound in his left arm. He is the son of the late Mr. George Smith, market gardener, of Beccles Road, well-known and highly respected local horticulturist who died only few days ago. Private Smith was present at his father's funeral on Wednesday of last week although is to be regretted that he did not arrive in time to see his father before his death.

Yarmouth Independent, Saturday 1ˢᵗ June 1918

Belton Parishioners who lost their lives in WW1:
Alfred John Arrowsmith, Ernest Brooks, William Mordon Carthew, William Robert Fuller, Percy Leonard Hayward, Claude Benjamin Horne, Albert Charles Howes, Alfred Coleman Kemp,

Sidney Robert Kemp, George Ambrose Mace,
Francis Robert Newark, George Alfred Saul,
Walter Alfred Shalders, James Henry Sharman
and Walter Edward Young.

Burgh Castle Parishioners who lost their lives in
WW1:
Arthur Sexton Bond, Albert Brackenbury, Robert
George Brooks, Edward (Senior) Casey, Edward
James Casey, James Casey, Lewis Collett,
William Flaxman, Thomas Frederick, Robert
George Harvey, George Robert Hewitt, Harry
Edward Hewitt, Joshua Hewitt, George Henry
High, John Johnson, George Samuel Meale,
James Martin Pembroke, Herbert Henry Perfect,
Bertie Francis Read, William Read and Robert
Samuel Saul.

1918 to 1939 the interwar years
Fred snr purchased Beech Farm, Belton at
auction in 1919, the land of which, surrounded
most of Pansy Villa market garden. The Sales
particulars for Beech Farm, Belton were as
follows:

- Lot 1, farmhouse, garden, outbuildings and 86a 0r 17p
- Lot 2, 1a 2r 9p known as Church *Pightle, Church Lane, Belton (*a small field, enclosure or paddock)
- Lot 2A, 27p of arable land on the north side of lot 2, Church Lane, Belton
- Lot 3, 13a 0r 3p of marsh, Belton
- Lot 4, 21a 1r 11p of plantation and heath land known as The Copse and Howards Common, Marsh Lane, Belton
- Lot 5, 4a 3r 21p of heath land, Marsh Lane

The auction was held at the Star Hotel, Great Yarmouth, by Auctioneers: Read, Stanford & Owles, of Beccles & Bungay. The land measurements were in pre-metric units, known as the Imperial System. The aforementioned land is listed in a, r and p which is acre, rood and perch.

30¼ square yards = 1 perch

40 perches = 1 rood

4 roods = 1 acre

Although the family now owned Beech Farm, the Market Garden at Pansy Villa was still extremely lucrative. Market gardeners who did not have glass houses could only grow for at the most 8 months of the year and were limited to produce such as cabbages, turnips, swedes and carrots etc. Glass houses facilitated the growing of produce which could not be grown outdoors and extended the growing season of produce such as lettuce. The number of glass houses at Pansy Villa increased dramatically in the first two decades of the 20th century to 21, covering an area of 22,559 square feet. This enabled the increase in production of tomatoes and cucumbers to meet the increasing demand and extending the season for cut flowers such as chrysanthemums, most of which were cut and dispatched to all corners of the UK by train, especially leading up to Christmas. On one day in 1930 Frud took a ton (224 boxes) of tomatoes to Yarmouth. Packing cucumbers all day, 130 boxes (1560 cucumbers). Tied 56 dozen (672) bunches of rhubarb. Tied chrysanthemums, sent 152 boxes (1800 bunches) away. The amount of produce generated under ½ an acre of glass is nothing short of astonishing.

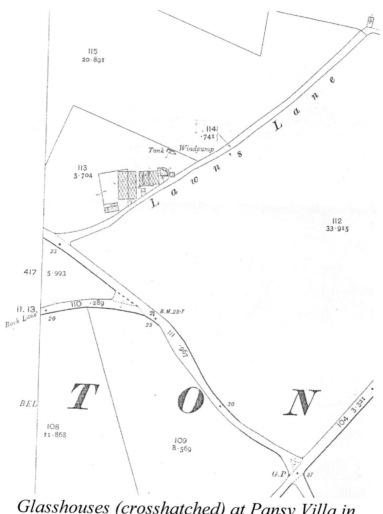

Glasshouses (crosshatched) at Pansy Villa in 1906

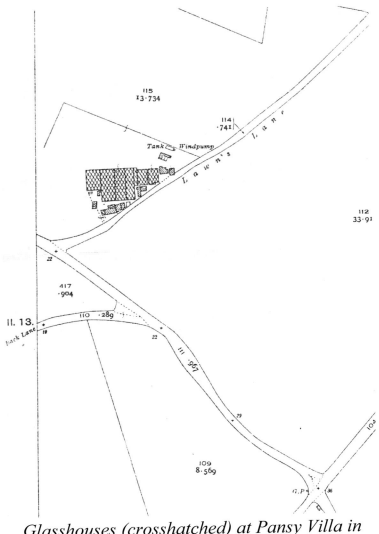

Glasshouses (crosshatched) at Pansy Villa in 1927

George Searby's Market Garden, Lound Rd, Browston
Courtesy of Mr Peter Searby

*Sam Beare's & Ted Searby's market gardens, Cherry
Lane, Browston*
Courtesy of Mr Tony Beare

Davy Beare's Market Garden, Browston Lane, Browston
Courtesy of Mrs Jane ~Kinge

Peter Botwright's Market Garden, Short Road, Browston
Courtesy of Mrs Jenny Hilling

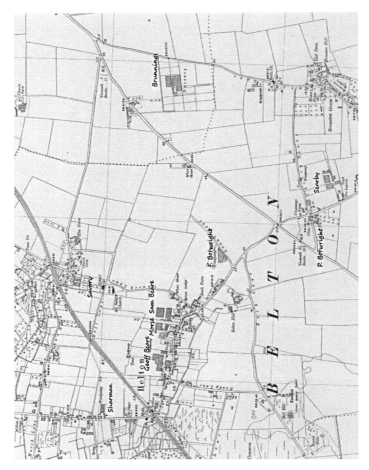

The previous photographs clearly show the number and extent of the glasshouses on a single market garden. There were numerous market gardens within the Parish of Belton and Browston in the early to mid-20th century as seen on the map of the Parish.

The last surviving market garden in the Parish
was at Browston, owned by Mr Sam Beare,
taken over by his two sons Tony and Ivor in the
1980s and in business up until 2017. The
following photograph shows Sam with his three
children on a Suffolk Punch horse with the
glasshouses in the background.

Sam Beare with his children on a Suffolk Punch
Courtesy of Mr Tony Beare

The glasshouses were heated by hot water within
cast iron pipes about a foot in diameter which
ran the length of each glasshouse, the water
being heated by 6 coal/coke fired

furnaces/boilers located in 'stoke holes' i.e. in an open pit below ground level to facilitate the convectional circulation of the heated water. The Robin Hood boiler, pictured, the last to be purchased at Pansy Villa, heated five glass houses.

The water source was from a 50ft deep, 5ft diameter, cylinder well which was then pumped, via a wind pump, into a holding tank (brick reservoir) measuring 40ft long by 12ft wide and 3ft deep holding 8,000 gallons of water, the tank being on ground slightly higher than the glasshouses to create the required gravity fed water pressure.

Coal/coke fired cast iron Robin Hood glasshouse furnace/boiler

Nick Moyes

(https://commons.wikimedia.org/wiki/File:Robin_Hood_Boiler,_Calke_Abbey_01.jpg), https://creativecommons.org/licenses/by-sa/4.0/legalcode

Wind
powered
water
pump
Ben Franske

The glass houses created a very lucrative competitive advantage, no doubt funding the purchase of nearby Beech Farm. Cucumbers could command a price of two shillings and six pence (12½ pence) which, when the average wage for an agricultural labourer was £1 and 8 shillings (£1.40p) per week, represented about 10% of the weekly wage. If the current average weekly wage is presumed to be £500, a cucumber would therefore cost £50! The cost of a cucumber was such due to the amount of labour intensive work involved in growing them and the cost of heating the glass houses.

Frud's sons Peter and Derek outside the glasshouses at Pansy Villa.

Frud in the cucumber house.

Beech Farm kept dairy cows, initially selling the milk wholesale to dairies and from the 1920s selling direct to the customer by establishing a milk round.

Milking Time
Guy Eric
(https://commons.wikimedia.org/wiki/File:Agriculture_in_Britain_during_the_First_World_War_Q27694.jpg), „Agriculture in Britain during the First World War Q27694", marked as public domain, more details on Wikimedia Commons: https://commons.wikimedia.org/wiki/Template:PD-UKGov

The Beech Farm milk round, delivered milk to residents, mainly in Gorleston. From the late 19th century and prior to the introduction of bottled milk, it was taken round in milk churns by horse and cart.

Frud's brothers, Roger and Harry with the milk churns on the horse drawn cart

Customers would bring a jug out to the cart and the milk was ladled from the churn and poured into the jug using a Milk Measuring Ladle, these comprised of ½ pint, 1 pint and 2 pint measures. Measuring ladles were used, up until the widespread delivery of bottled milk after World War II. The ladles were usually made from tinplate with a curved metal handle so that it could hang on the side of the milk churn.

Milk churn measure ladles

The instigation of the milk round appears to have been forced upon the business. Before the round came into being, the milk was sold wholesale to a Mr Cooper, a typical delivery being 35 gallons. Frud's diary entry for February 1923 states:

"Sat. 17th. Went to Gorleston with milk, Cooper say he will not pay. Went to see if I could get a milk round in the

afternoon. Sun. 18th. Roger, Henry and I went on a milk round, sold out. Mon. 19th. Henry and Roger went to Gorleston with milk. Went to Yarmouth to have names put on serving cans and requested to be a retail milkman. Tues. 20th. Went with Henry and Roger with milk, sold out. Wed. 21st. Father and Mother (Fred snr and Lucy) went to lawyer's to see about milk."

Post WW2 the milk was delivered in Bottles, note the card insert/stopper, and imprinted on the bottle was:

Botwright & Sons
Beech Farm Dairy
Belton
From our own herd

Frud's Diaries

Frud kept a diary from 1923 to 1944. The entries were extremely concise to the degree that some of the content can be difficult to comprehend. Nevertheless, the diary does illustrate some of the farming and horticultural methodologies, old varieties of vegetables and flowers and the lifestyle during this period.

Staff

Fred senior's workforce predominantly included his six children and their spouses, grandchildren, plus some men from the village.

FAMILY: Fred snr, Lucy Snr, Frud, Anne, Joy, Herbert, Maggie, Henry, Lucy, Walter, Harry, Ethel, Roger, Jenny, Marjorie, Peter, Derek, Jack, (18 people)

Back row L to R, Frud's brother-in-law Herbert Bond, Frud's brothers Roger and Harry, Jack Coleman, Cleggs Easter, Frud's brother-in-law Henry Saul, Front row, Dinker Easter, and Frud's future son-in-law Bertie (Jellicoe) Saul.

There were many other people who worked for Fred senior, mentioned in Frud's diaries, which he kept from 1922 to 1944, namely: Frank Austin, Lion Balls, Charlie Beare, Sidney Beare, Davy Beare, Harry Blackstone, Snip Brackenbury, Leslie Brooks, Albert Casey, Arthur Casey, Jack Coleman, Harry Chilvers, Billy Coe, Tiger Durrant, Phil Durrant, Tom Durrant, Cleggs Easter, Dinker Easter, George Flatt, Jack Flatt, Billo Grimmer, Bob Guyton,

Frank Horne, Lawrence Horne, Bob Holt, Jack
Holt, Jack Howe, Arthur Moy, H. Oakley, Alfred
Perfect, Ernest Perfect, Hali Perfect, Pinny
Perfect, Bob Pye, Charlie Reynolds, Bertie Saul,
Grayson Saul, Harold Saul, Barnard Saunders,
Charlie Sharman, Sam Sharman, Old Steward,
Sykes Wakefield, Sam Vincent, Old Vincent,
Billy Wilson, Jack Wilson, Tom Woodrow,
Alder and his son, Bob, Bobby, Brookes,
Canham, Danny, Dewney, Drit, Dudley,
Duffield, Gill, Ginger, Higgins, Knights, Macie,
Nicholls, Pat, Percy, Pettingill, Old Tom,
Tommy (71 people)

The number of people that worked on the market
garden and farm is quite staggering but in the
early part of the 20th century the lack of
mechanisation and the subsequent labour-
intensive nature of the work required this large
workforce. The aforementioned people were not
employed concurrently, staff started and left
work fairly regularly, either they got a better
offer of pay, or didn't like the work, and men left
to join the forces both prior to and during WW2.
1931 Bertie Saul left to join Navy. 1932

Snip Brackenbury left for the Merchant Service. Frud's son Peter joined the Navy in 1940 and his cousin Jack in 1943. 1933 Dinker left after being with us for over 30 years.

One character who worked for the business appeared to have an aversion to water, personal hygiene, tonsorial participation and the cutting of his finger and toe nails, was Phil Durrant, apparently, you could smell him coming before you could see him. He is the one who stuck his shotgun up the chimney and fired it from this precarious position when a skein of geese went over his house resulting in food for the table and money in the pocket from the sale of the geese.

Another character who served in WW1 had 'shell shock' if asked to barrow something to a particular location, he would set off, continuously humming to himself and just kept going, further instructions via shouting were required to get him to stop. This anecdote is both humorous and sad, but shell shock was real. Today it would be classified as post-traumatic stress disorder (PTSD). It is a reaction to the intensity of the bombardment that WW1 soldiers experienced in the trenches and manifested itself in various guises. In WW2 the phrase was coined the 'thousand-yard stare' used to describe the blank, unfocused gaze of soldiers who have become emotionally detached from the horrors around them.

Frud records in his diary: *Thursday 12th June 1931 this week the wages fall 2/- per man in Suffolk.* Agricultural wage rates had legally established minimum wages. The Agricultural Wages (Regulation) Act 1924 established a base rate of pay for agricultural workers. In early 1930 this was £1 11s (shillings) 8d (pence) for a week of just over 50 hours, or roughly a shilling (5p) an hour. This rate declined slightly in the early 1930s, falling as low as £1 10s 8d in 1933-4, but had increased again by the end of the decade, standing at £1 19s 5$^{1}/_{2}$d (just under £2) by October 1939. 6th Feb 1942 *gave all the men their holidays.* During WW2 all staff worked until 9pm, such was the demand for food.

Farming and Market Gardening
Cultivating, muck spreading/fertilising, ploughing, harrowing, planting, hoeing, harvesting and animal husbandry were frequent and common jobs and there were many other labour intensive tasks. Many tasks involved the use of man powered implements i.e. the spade, fork, hoe, rake, some were semi mechanised e.g. the push hoe and the push seed drill.

Push Hoe
Courtesy of Mr Tony Beare

Push Seed Drill
Courtesy of Mr Tony Beare

Planet were the leading company for 'push' implements. The two photographs show the push hoe and the push seed drill but there were numerous attachments that could be purchased e.g. cultivator, rake, plough, harrow, ridger et al.

Up until the 1930s the main form of power used to pull agricultural implements was the horse.

A single furrow horse-drawn plough.
Smirkybec (https://commons.wikimedia.org/wiki/File:Irish_horse_drawn_plough.jpg),
https://creativecommons.org/licenses/by-sa/4.0/legalcode

Agnes Deans Cameron
(https://commons.wikimedia.org/wiki/File:Man_ploughing_with_a_horses-drawn_plough_ (S2004-912_LS).jpg), https://creativecommons.org/licenses/by-sa/4.0/legalcode

100

(https://commons.wikimedia.org/wiki/File:Agriculture_in_Britain_during_the_First_
World_War_Q54601.jpg), „Agriculture in Britain during the First World War
Q54601", marked as public domain, more details on Wikimedia Commons:
https://commons.wikimedia.org/wiki/Template:PD-UKGov

Nicholls Horace
*(https://commons.wikimedia.org/wiki/File:Agriculture_in_Britain_during_the_First_*
World_War_Q30655.jpg), „Agriculture in Britain during the First World War
Q30655", marked as public domain, more details on Wikimedia Commons:
https://commons.wikimedia.org/wiki/Template:PD-UKGov

Harrowing and drilling seed with horses
Ministry of Information Photo Division Photographer
(https://commons.wikimedia.org/wiki/File:Agriculture_in_Britain-
_Life_on_Mount_Barton_Farm,_Devon,_England,_1942_D9916.jpg), „Agriculture
in Britain- Life on Mount Barton Farm, Devon, England, 1942 D9916", marked as
public domain, more details on Wikimedia Commons:
https://commons.wikimedia.org/wiki/Template:PD-UKGov

When horses were the main source of power on every farm, it was the tip-cart, rather than the wagon which was the most common vehicle for anyone farming with horses. Simple construction two wheels, a tipping body and shafts. The tumbrel, or tip cart, played a vital role in the day-to-day running of a farm. On practical grounds, it was simple in construction and therefore cheap, it can tip its load on to the ground, saving time in handling and it is very manoeuvrable in narrow lanes and farm yards. A tumbrel was used to cart manure from the livestock sheds and stables to the fields and bring sugar beet or turnips back to the farm. It was slightly inclined backwards and had a slotted tailgate for ease of unloading, some also had a mechanism which when released simply tumbled the load off the cart i.e. when carting muck (manure) this would be dumped in piles on the field and then spread by farm labourers with muck forks. The great advantage of the cart over the waggon is its ability to quickly tip its load. Before tipping the cart the tailboard is removed. Then the tipping lever, or other mechanism to secure the front of the cart body to the shafts, is released. The wheels were made from three different types of wood - oak for the spokes, ash for the fellers (round sections of the wheel) and elm for the hubs.

Frud's diary entries include: *Carted the last of the swedes off with three tumblrels. Herbert, Lawrence and I went to Buxton's with two tumbrels to get leaves. Carting soil off Turnpike field all day, four tumbrel loads. Carted beet all day, utilising four tumbrels a total of 200 loads. 1942 Henry varnished the tumbrel, the first one to have rubbers (tyres) on the farm.*

The Tumbrel or tip cart, using a crome to pull the muck off the cart.

A tumbrel with a Suffolk Punch horse.
Courtesy of George Pratt and Suffolk horse Colony Viceroy 2nd

The Suffolk Punch registry is the oldest English breed society. The first known mention of the Suffolk Punch is in William Camden's Britannia, published in 1586, in which he describes a working horse of the eastern counties of England that is easily recognisable as the Suffolk Punch. Local farmers developed the Suffolk Punch for farm work, for which they needed a horse with power, stamina, health, longevity, and docility, and they bred the Suffolk to comply with these needs.

Other breeds of Heavy or Draught horses which were used in the UK include Shire, Percheron and Clydesdale.

Suffolk Punch Stallion

Suffolkp at English Wikipedia
(https://commons.wikimedia.org/wiki/File:A_Suffolk_stallion.jpg), „A Suffolk stallion", marked as public domain, more details on Wikimedia Commons: https://commons.wikimedia.org/wiki/Template:PD-user

Gradually in the early 20th century, and hastened by the demand for food and need for improved efficiency during WW2, the horse was replaced by the tractor. Mechanisation of the farm equalled efficiency. In the 19th century wheat and corn were mowed by men with scythes and then came the reaper binder. The cereal crop was cut and tied but still had to be threshed.

A horse powered Reaper-Binder

Lands Department, Survey of Lands Branch, Photographic Branch (https://commons.wikimedia.org/wiki/File:Queensland_State_Archives_3930_Harvesting_wheat_with_horse_drawn_reapers_and_binders_Canning_Downs_near_Warwick_16_November_1894.png), „Queensland State Archives 3930 Harvesting wheat with horse drawn reapers and binders Canning Downs near Warwick 16 November 1894", marked as public domain, more details on Wikimedia Commons: https://commons.wikimedia.org/wiki/Template:PD-Australia

Jan 1935 got 1½ ton of coal for threshing, 30/- per ton. Beare's engine came to thresh stack of oats and barley, thrashed out 110 coombs of oats and 15 of barley.

Steam powered threshing

https://s0.geograph.org.uk/geophotos/05/52/41/5524150_29fd8cf0.jpg
Evelyn Simak (CC BY-SA 2.0)

A steam engine connected by a large canvas belt was used to power the threshing of oats and barley, the grain being packaged in coomb hessian sacks. A coomb was a measure of volume equating to 16 stone (100kg) which had to be manhandled once filled. Most farm workers carried these 16 stone sacks of grain on their backs, the carrying of which involved both an acquired knack to get them on their back as well as a great deal of strength.

"Gave all the cows half a pint of raw linseed", a protein supplement containing a large amount of digestible nutrients, increasing milk yield and improving the fat profile of the milk, also beneficial for the making of butter.

Chaff cutting (using a mechanical device for cutting straw or hay into small pieces before being mixed together with other forage and fed to horses and cattle to aid the animal's digestion)

Hand cranked chaff cutter

Panhard

Frud frequently went down to marsh to tend the cows, to make sure they were alright and had not got stuck in a dyke etc. This task was undertaken on one day when he had a sickness and diarrhoea bug. In the middle of the marsh he was suddenly aware that he needed to go to the toilet, there being no hedges on the marsh he hurriedly made his way towards a carr (a wooded fen in a waterlogged terrain on the edge of the marshes) to relieve himself. As he briskly made his way, coughing and sneezing simultaneously with one hand over each orifice, a violent sneeze caused him to lose control of his bodily functions and he soiled himself, simultaneously, his false teeth flew out of his mouth and landed smack bang in the middle of a cow pat. This evoked great hilarity when his mishap was recounted.

Sat. 24th Oct 1936 The Scotch herring girls out on strike. The fisher girls successfully acquired an increase in wages from 10d to 1s per barrel. The fisher girls gutted the herring and packed the herring in barrels of salt and ice for export. In 1925, the predominantly Scottish herring industry in Great Yarmouth, were represented by 757 boats and 4,000 fisher girls. By 1936 the figures were nearer 460 and 2,000.

The fish guts (gips) were much sort after by farmers and growers as a fertiliser, prior to artificial fertilisers. When the gips were spread on the land they hurriedly needed to be ploughed in, as, almost instantaneously, the field was inundated with seagulls.

Hedge cutting not only maintained a good thick hedge and animal barrier but the 'quicks' prickly hawthorn and blackthorn were used to spread on the land prior to the fish guts to impede the seagulls eating this valuable fertiliser. The quicks were also used in the production of cucumber nests a mixture of quicks, gorse, leaves and soil within which to grow the cucumbers.

23rd Oct 1934 A glut of herring (supply exceeding demand), *bought about one hundred crans at 3/- to 3/6 per cran.*

*Herbert and Walter ploughing the
herring in.*

A cran or herring barrel was a unit of capacity
for fresh herring equivalent to approximately 40
imperial gallons or 180 litres, typically
containing about 1200 fish, but could vary from
700 to 2500. Spreading whole herring on the
field as opposed to the guts resulted in many
villagers visiting the field collecting the herring
to eat themselves, as this was a valuable source
of protein and a treat for those who couldn't
always afford to buy them.

Jack Coleman was hoeing on the field opposite
the newly built council houses on Sandy Lane.
He noticed that a woman was at the bedroom
window observing him and his fellow workers,
this continued for some time, every time he
looked she was still there staring at the men, he
thought I've had enough of this, I'll give her
something to look at, and subsequently dropped
his trousers and shew her his bottom.

Agricultural salt appears to have been used on the land as a pesticide, herbicide and as a fertiliser. This is peculiar as salt is generally considered to contaminate soil and yet a nutrient for a number of crops, particularly those with 'maritime' origins as their ancestors grew near the sea. The most high profile of these crops is sugar beet. Sodium is also recommended for use on crops such as asparagus, celery and carrots.

The glass houses were the most labour intensive side of the business, many of the jobs on the farm could be undertaken with horses, whereas in the glasshouses it was mainly manual.

The benefits of the glasshouse enabled crops to be grown in the colder months and thus the growing season extended. This enabled produce to be available when the usual season had finished, resulting in demand exceeding supply and subsequently the achievement of very good prices for the produce.

Harvesting and Packing

From January through to March glass houses were used for growing rhubarb. This was extremely beneficial for cash flow as income could be acquired when there was little other produce to sell. *March 28th 1923 Tied 64 dozen (768) bunches of rhubarb. Wed. 4th. Tied 30 dozen rhubarb for Lowestoft."* 18th March 1927 *"Last of the rhubarb, 234 dozen (2808 bunches).* The rhubarb was not only sold locally i.e. in Yarmouth and Lowestoft but also sent by train to Newcastle, Birmingham, Glasgow, Leeds and London.

Varieties of vegetables grown were: Tomatoes - Kondine Red, Cucumbers - Worthing Supreme, Potatoes - Eclipse, King Edward and Sharp's Express, Beetroot - Champion Globe, Swede - Giant Tankard, most of these are no longer available. Other crops grown included: - oats, barley, cow cabbage, spring cabbage, marrow, kale, radishes, lettuce, kohlrabi, turnips, broccoli, runner beans, strawberries, sugar beet and more.

The cut flowers and greenery grown included: - sweet peas, wallflowers, privet, stocks, asters, cornflowers, chrysanthemums, gladioli, iris, carnations, pinks, roses, marguerites, scabious, statice, helichrysum, gypsophila, michaelmas daisies, gaillardias, pyrethrums, cats tail, rhodanthemums, thistles, chinese lanterns, bachelors buttons ,marigolds, calendula, honesty, peonies, montbretia, lillies, aquilegia, sweet williams, dahlias, sea lavender and sea holly.

The main cut flower grown was chrysanthemum both outdoor and under glass, the latter being extremely lucrative in the month of December. Varieties grown included: - Nagoya, Queen, Brooke, Sauce, Freeman Groch's Crimson, Cranford Yellow, Fromfield Yellow, Ipswich Beauty, Triumphant, Globe, December Bronze, Lord Brooke, Yellow Mass, Romance, Lance, Nurse Cavell, Heston, Valet, Crimson Baldock, Josephine, Romance, Blanc Popay, Phoenix, La Pope, Harvester, Balcombe Beauty, Conquest, Goldfinder, Mrs. Humphrey, Ra, Jean, Ada Brooker, Favourite, Friendly Rival, Page, Algones Bronze, Sanford, Yellow Glory, Early Pink, Fiona and May Wallace.

Indoor (glass house) Chrysanthemums
Courtesy of Mr Tony Beare

Outdoor Chrysanthemums, stuck and tied at
Waveney Nurseries, Belton

Courtesy of Mr Tony Beare

Grace Beare cutting sweet peas

Courtesy of Mrs Jane Applegate

Cut flowers were the main item of produce sent away by train to Newcastle, Birmingham, Glasgow, Leeds and London. - *Tied, packed and sent pansies, gladiolas and marguerites to Glasgow. Friday 18th July 1924 cut flowers all day, 75 dozen (900) bunches. Cutting 'thicks' from Belton marshes* (bull rushes / sedge) used to incorporate with bunched flowers.

A worrying time for the business, being reliant on the train to despatch their produce, was the general strike, which Frud notes in his diary. *May 3rd 1926 the strike have started there should be a general strike at 12 tonight. Wednesday May 12th 1926 the strike finished, the railway men will not go back.* The railwaymen faced the most ferocious anti-union backlash in the aftermath of the strike. The conditions on which they were to be re-employed and subsequent negotiation resulted in some railway employees not getting back to work for six months after the end of the strike.

Mechanisation

In Frud's early life the steam locomotive and steam traction engine were established but the main means of power and transportation was the Horse, to ride, or with trap, tumbrel and cart, to plough, cultivate and harrow, and to transport produce.

Frud, left, with his father Fred Snr and horses

Brenda, Deany, 'Diamond & Tom', Bob Beckett
The old and the new, circa 1950, last use of
heavy horses in Belton, Frud's future daughter-
in-law driving the tractor.

In 1924 Frud and his Father went to Rodney
Road, Gt. Yarmouth to Pure Ice Cream
Company's auction where they appear to have
bought their first lorry for the princely sum of
£16. This was then washed, painted and
varnished. May 1931 Frud went to Yarmouth,
he had his first lesson on a recently purchased
motor truck and brought it home. The next day
Anne and Frud went to market with the motor
for the first time. It would appear that Frud was
not the most proficient driver having frequent

accidents and mishaps with the motor lorry. His diary entry states *Frud, Anne, Lucy, Peter, Derek and Marjorie drove into a lamp standard near Woolworths,* note they all drove into the lamp standard but Frud was driving!

Travelling round an acute right angled bend when entering Loddon, Frud turned the lorry over carrying a load of cinders, they went all over the gardens, which were well below the road level of the houses bordering the roads.

1934 Sold F. Skipper the little lorry for £9. Another motor lorry was purchased in1934 which was converted into a cattle float. Henry started to make the cattle float for the lorry. Harry Payne (Blacksmith) making the irons for the cattle float.

1935 Father, Harry and I bought a tractor and plough £122. Henry harrowing the Home field with tractor, it goes very well indeed.

Early steel-wheel tractor ploughing

Unknown author
*(https://commons.wikimedia.org/wiki/File:Agriculture_in_Britain_during_the_First_
World_War_Q54602.jpg), „Agriculture in Britain during the First World War
Q54602", marked as public domain, more details on Wikimedia Commons:
https://commons.wikimedia.org/wiki/Template:PD-UKGov*

Disc harrowing

*Alison Phillips (https://commons.wikimedia.org/wiki/File:FordsonFarmacp.jpg),
„FordsonFarmacp", marked as public domain, more details on Wikimedia
Commons: https://commons.wikimedia.org/wiki/Template:PD-user*

*Sam & Tony Beare carting and stacking straw
bales 1973*
Courtesy of Mr Tony Beare

No one appeared to like Fred Snr, the men called him 'Ole Thick' presumably due to his thick set build. When a truck got stuck in mud down the marsh and the men were summoned to free the trapped vehicle, stifled laughter ensued when the back wheels spun and showered Ole Thick from top to bottom in mud, although he did not see the funny side of it.

The Yarmouth–Beccles line was a railway line which linked the Suffolk market town of Beccles with the Norfolk coastal resort of Yarmouth. Forming part of the East Suffolk Railway, the line was opened in 1859 and closed 100 years later in 1959. The line ran from Beccles to Aldeby, Haddiscoe High Level, St Olave's, Belton and Yarmouth Southtown, with sidings and access to the wharves. Villagers could get on the train at Belton and go direct, i.e. no changes of train, to London. For the market garden and indeed all the other market gardens in Belton, the train greatly expanded their market, enabling produce to be transported quickly to all parts of the UK. Fred regularly used the train to travel to the Auctions at Yarmouth and Beccles as it was more comfortable and quicker than travelling by horse and cart.

Non Farming activities

The work on the market garden and farm was not all about animal husbandry and growing crops, the upkeep of the infrastructure was also continuous; carpentry, glazing, bricklaying and engineering skills were required to undertake the building and maintenance of glasshouses, the repairing of tools and implements, stock fences and gates, hedge-laying, the dredging of deeks (dykes) the drawings (sediment) then used to fill the holes in the marsh track. *Dinker made and painted four Ash *whippletrees, Dinker and Knights thatched the top of the barn, Knights and Herbert thatched the stable roof, Dinker made hovels into boxes for horses, Dinker building a house for cooling the milk in, Herbert, Harry, Dinker, Dudley and I went into the back lane to trim the hedge for stock bottoms.* *a pivoted or swinging bar to which the traces, or tugs, of a harness are fastened, and by which a carriage, a plough, or the like, is drawn. The skills which many of the men possessed was astounding, as in the expression 'he can turn his hand to anything'.

Out and About

Buying

Frud's working life was not confined to the market garden and farm, he visited numerous auctions and farm sales, purchasing agricultural and horticultural equipment, and livestock e.g. chickens, ducks, pigs, horses and cows.

Went with Bond and Father to Burgh St. Peter about bull; went with Father to Beccles in Hewitt's motor; went over to Haddiscoe to get watercress roots; went to Primrose's, Abbots Manor, Kirby Cane, bought two cows, £17 each; went to Shadingfield, bought cow for £20 10s and three heifers for £9 5s; went to Beccles, bought brindle and white calf £23 15s.

Frud visited various suppliers to purchase seed, bought three cwt Scotch seed, King Edward 15s per cwt; went to see Gordon at Herringfleet Hall to get tomato seeds; lucerne seed from Cannell's of Loddon. He also visited suppliers to purchase and collect, fertiliser, soda of nitrate, sulphur of ammonia, lime, salt, leaves, cattle cake (feed), wood, paint, tools, coke, coal, glass, hessian corn sacks, raffia, cement, barbed wire, flower boxes, etc. Frud also purchased bulbs from Holland. Bill Van Hort visited Frud at Pansy Villa where an order was placed.

Collection and haulage of manure pig, horse, cow and guano (The accumulated excrement of seabirds, seals, or cave-dwelling bats. As a manure, guano is a highly effective fertilizer due to its exceptionally high content of nitrogen, phosphate and potassium: nutrients essential for plant growth.)

Went to Herringfleet Hall for leaves, chestnut stakes and poles and Hazel wood for to put in the bottom of the skeps, Tom got a load of furze (gorse) bushes. Roger and Henry went to Wright's at Toft Monks after 40 bundles of pea sticks. Went and got chain harrow from Jarvis at Lound, went to Oulton Foundry after links for cleaner, plough fittings and plough shear breast.

Jewsons was visited on a regular basis e.g. after load of scantlings and spars for the glasshouse, wood for the hovel (an open shed), wood for cow mangers, wire nails, pitch pine slats 45s and two cwt linseed 28s, red lead, etc.

Auctions

Frud travelled to many auctions locally, mainly to buy but also to sell. There were many auctioneers who held regular 'sales' which were attended but also auctions were frequently held on farms. *Went to Amis's auction at Browston; went to auction near the pub at Mutford; went to Holly Farm County Council auction, bought harrow carriage; Anne went to Slater's auction; Jary's auction day, bought a big roll £6 15s; Bond's auction; went to two auctions on Hales Green, bought little red roan heifer £18; went to Harrison's auction; went to Bullock's auction, bought a cow, cultivator, lime and spare stubbing tools; went to auction at Stockton just past the Black Boy; went to marsh letting at St Olaves Bell and hired two marshes 40s & 25s per acre; went to Bungay May Fair, bought a red roan mare £24; took two cows, two calves, a bullock, and ponies to Mile's auction; took fat pig to Mile's sale and bought two rabbits; Father and I went to*

Flixton Old Hall auction; Jack and I took Charlie the bullock up to Maddison's sale £29 15s; went to Yarmouth sale with Father; went to Yarmouth sale, Bond sold nine cows; went to Matthew Mann's auction; Father went to Jack Buck's auction; Father and I went to auction at Thurlton, bought cow and calf £51; Father, Herbert and I went to Patrick's auction at Haddiscoe; went with Father to Wittrick's auction at Bungay, bought their heifer Strawberry, £18 10s; Father and I drove to Loddon sale, bought two black heifers, paid £13 5s; went to Way's auction, bought Lily for £26 and Roger a gun; went to J. Rolfe's auction at Ashby, bought fowls house; Father and I went to Beckett's auction, Burgh Castle, bought fowls house; Joe Tailor's auction at Herringfleet; Father and I went to Damby's auction, Carpenters Yard farm, Somerleyton, we bought heifer and calf £17 10s; Father and I went to Woods auction, Baker Street, Gorleston; Went

with Father and Harry to Martin
Hammond's auction, bought Daisy a
black and white cow £35; Father went
to Wreaks auction at St. Olaves, bought
some Lily of the Valley; Cleggs and
Harry went to Tombland Fair; Father
and I went to Dye's auction, bought
some Bonemeal; Went to Hall's, Gapton
Hall auction, bought basic slag (for
meadows); Went to Hook's auction,
bought two turkeys 26s; Father, Harry
and I went to Rushmere's auction at
Thurlton, bought copper kettle 3s 6d;
Went to Walker's auction, Welcome
Farm, Burgh Castle; Father and I went
to Castle's sale, bought five year old
horse £28 17s 6d; Stannard's auction
day, bought tumbrel and small seed
drill; took two cows to Yarmouth sale,
Topaz £14 and Blossom £20 15s; went to
Mile's sale took the red bull it made £19
10s, Thursday 11th February 1926 went
to 'Oak Wreck' sale from the drifter 'Lily
of the valley' at St. Olaves.

Deliveries

Frud undertook deliveries of the market garden and farm's produce in and around Lothingland, Great Yarmouth and Lowestoft, and to Belton Railway station for customers further afield. He delivered milk from the cows to a wholesaler in Gorleston, pigs to W. Beck the butcher in Belton, cows, chickens and ducks to Yarmouth sale and Read & Owl's sale at Beccles. *Went to Lowestoft took Soanes 333 tomato plants, delivered La Porte a ton of potatoes, went to Blundeston with statice. Went with horse Tommy and cart to Yarmouth with load of broccoli. Went to Lowestoft, 72 cues, tomatoes, strawberries, flowers and 12 dozen Cabbages. Went to Lowestoft with cues, sold 40 dozen.* Most Saturdays produce was sold on Yarmouth Market. *Joy and I went to Yarmouth market with Sweet-Peas, cues, tomatoes, flowers and strawberries.* Frud's deliveries were not always straight forward, on one occasion, when delivering sprouts to Yarmouth, he lost his way coming home in the fog.

Entertainment

Herbert, Joy, Anne, Peter, Marjorie and I went for a drive in the Governess Cart as far as Hopton Hart.

A Governess Cart

It would be reasonable to assume that travel would be limited to within the surrounding villages and Great Yarmouth, but Frud regularly travelled into Suffolk, by horse and trap, and later to Diss and Ipswich and numerous villages within Suffolk by truck or train.

Visits to London, were not unusual, either by charabanc or train. Frud could catch the train at Belton and travel direct to London, alas this line was a victim of the infamous Beeching cuts. Frud and his family also regularly attended the Norfolk Show, Suffolk Show, Mutford and Lothingland Show held at Beccles, the Bungay May Fair and Benacre Park races. The Norfolk and Suffolk shows did not have a permanent venue at this time, and each year, each show was held at a different location around the county.

Despite living in a rural location the family were not lacking recreation. Walking was a favourite pastime on a Sunday afternoon within the village or to neighbouring villages such as Lound and Fritton. Lound Run was a picturesque destination for a walk with the lake, woodland and especially when the Rhododendrons were in bloom.

Lound Run circa 1910

Lound Run circa 1955

Courtesy of Mr Tony Beare

13th March 1927 Frud bought his first bicycle. Anne took Peter on her bicycle over to Haddiscoe (a round trip of 10 miles with a young child, presumably in a seat on the back of the bike). Letter writing and receipt was a favourite pastime. Frud first heard a wireless (radio) in 1925 and purchased a wireless in 1932. Frud travelled regularly to Haddiscoe, 5 miles away, to visit Anne's family, in the early part of the 20th century by pony and trap and by the 1930s by motor vehicle. As well as visiting relatives, relatives also visited: Sunday 16th August 1931 Cousin Fred (son of Fred's brother John) his wife Harriett and daughter Freda came from South Shields last night. Went down to the King's Head, three Fred Botwrights together. Cousin Fred, Harriett and Freda stayed for tea. Frud competed in a ploughing match at Burgh Castle and won a prize. Shooting was both a leisure activity and provided food for the table, and it got rid of pigeons and rabbits which decimated the crops. Frud also 'went to flight' meaning standing in Belton Pit wood in the morning or evening shooting ducks as they flew in and out of Fritton Lake and he 'went rabbiting' using ferrets. Another leisure activity which put food on the table: *Bertie, Dinker, Jack, Roger, Harry and I went to Burgh marshes after eels.* Angling was also undertaken: *Charlie and I went fishing down Blocka Run.*

A young Tony Beare, fishing at Blocka Run
By kind permission of Mr Tony Beare

After the First World War Frud was heavily involved with the British Legion and the Ex-Servicemen's Club who held regular parades to church and around the neighbouring villages, usually lead by some local dignitary e.g. Captain Crossley/Sir Thomas Jackson. *11th January 1926 went down to Institute at night time ex-servicemen's club. 5th February 1926 last night there was an ex-servicemen's club smoker. 13th March 1926 went last night to the committee meeting down the Kings Head for ex-servicemen's club. 8th April 1926 went to whist drive up at the school for ex-servicemen. 14th November 1926 parade of about 50 ex-servicemen round the village, led by May Arnold. I went down to X-Servicemen's smoker at night time. X-Servicemen's fete held on Bland's meadow for the first time. 27th May 1927 went down to Kings Head at night time, ex-servicemen's proposed a whist drive for a church window in memory of Rev. Albert Reynolds. 28th June 1931 X-Serviceman's dedication on the rectory lawn, four bands played. Jan 7th 1933 The X-Serviceman's dinner at the Kings Head, about 100 sat down.*

The village provided two pubs, one of which had a much used bowls green. Frud, going to the pub, couldn't find any clean underwear, dropping his trousers in the Tavern stating, "I'm lovely and warm" as he stands there in Anne's long legged silk bloomers. Most customers would leave the pub having had a few pints and as the cold air hit them, naturally they needed to urinate, without hesitation they would relieve themselves wherever they were as was the way in a rural village, but this habit was deemed improper and it was reported and raised at the Parish Council meeting. On one occasion, walking home from the pub with his brother-in-law, Frud suddenly disappeared behind a field hedge, reappearing he declared 'bad beer'.

As with many pubs there could be rowdiness, Frud reports: *"Stopped at Ives (Railway Tavern) E. Buck very noisy, pulled his coat off at me."*

*Belton Railway Tavern bowls club circa 1930s,
Frud and his brother Roger centre front.*

Frud appears to have enjoyed his bowls, it regularly appears in his diary:

Went to a bowling match at Herringfleet Hall. Went down to Ives (Railway Tavern) for bowls, played G.E.R. (Great Eastern Railways). Played L.N.E.R. bowls club and beat them. Henry and I went down to Ives to play bowls with the Halfway House, we lost. Went in Ives's motor to Rumbold Arms to play bowls. Henry and I went to Ives bowling, I won a barrow. Went down to Ives for a game of bowls against the Tramway.

The Village Institute offered whist, phat and beetle drives, music, concerts, billiards and amateur dramatic plays. *Nov 28th 1934 Went to a concert at the Institute. Acted in a farce called Widecombe Fair, I was the old grey mare.*

The Belton Institute and Reading Room, erected by public subscription in 1885 at a cost of £300.
Belton Community Hall in Station Road South
cc-by-sa/2.0 - © Evelyn Simak - geograph.org.uk/p/1664893

Perhaps the Village Institute's greatest claim to fame is that it was the venue for Sir John Mills' first public performance. The young John, dressed in a sailor suit danced a horn pipe at a concert organised by his father. It went down well and drew great applause. Interviewed on 'Desert Island Discs', nearly 90 years later, Sir John said that it was his first taste of show business that made him want to become an actor.

Frud and Anne also visited the Conservative Club in Gorleston to attend whist drives and socials. Anne attended a whist drive at Burgh Castle and the Liberal whist drive. Henry and Maggie came up to tea and a game of cards. Playing cards it appears was very much in vogue at this time and a means of socialising between friends and family both at home and at local clubs.

Gorleston has a fabulous beach and Frud and his family visited this quite often in the summer, to paddle or swim.

L-R Frud, Anne, Peter et al on the beach

This locale also hosted Fossett's circus in the late 1920s. Fossett's circus was established in 1852 and is still in business today in Ireland.

Gorleston Beach was also the venue for Alan Cobham's 1935 National Aviation Day Display Tour of the UK (14th July 1935) taking off and landing at Wheatcroft Farm Aerodrome, Gorleston, Great Yarmouth; a Civil Landing Ground becoming a Temporary Aerodrome at times. Some of the planes flying in the display are as follows:

PAutogiro

De_Havilland_DH82_Tiger_Moth

Lockheed Vega
Unlisted by ASC History Office
(https://commons.wikimedia.org/wiki/File:Detroit_Y1C-12.JPG), „Detroit Y1C-12",
marked as public domain, more details on Wikimedia Commons:
https://commons.wikimedia.org/wiki/Template:PD-US

Great Yarmouth offered variety shows, 'the pictures' (cinema), the Pleasure Beach, the Annual Easter Fair and boxing at the Hippodrome. The Hippodrome was built in 1903 by the legendary circus showman George Gilbert. As well as traditional circus shows, Lillie Langtry sang, Little Tich clowned, Max Miller joked, Houdini escaped, the world's finest clowns and circus personalities performed.

Hippodrome Great Yarmouth circa 1920s

Norwich Hippodrome was also visited By Frud where variety shows and plays were hosted.

Norwich Hippodrome circa 1900

Frud and his family also travelled much further afield including London, visiting Whipsnade Zoo and London Zoo, and in September 1925 Frud went to Wembley. Frud and Anne went on a trip by charabanc to London Zoo. Frud decided he would take some 'carly cues' with him to feed the monkeys at the zoo but the cues didn't get that far. Inevitably the charabanc would make frequent stops at the local hostelries, which suited Frud, to say he liked a drink is an understatement. One of these stops brought Frud into contact with several young ladies, always the gentleman, Frud innocently and generously offered these ladies the cucumbers, as they were indeed a rare treat and expensive, little did Frud realise that these ladies were harlots!

At Home

Anne worked on the market garden, cutting and tying flowers, picking fruit, weeding etc. but also had to undertake the house work, cooking cleaning, washing, ironing etc. all of these tasks were hard work and time consuming. In addition to these tasks she also undertook a lot of preserving and pickling, making piccalilli and preserving beans in salt water, pickling onions and making jams, no freezers then! All crops had a definitive season and preserving these enabled their consumption throughout the year. It does however make one wonder where she found the time to undertake all these tasks and work on the market garden as well. Without a minute to live Anne would inevitably be rushing to get things done, resulting in the odd breakage of a cup or bowl, her anger at the breakage would be exacerbated by Frud saying 'well Anne, whatever did you do that for?'

The local postman was a character, oblivious to the newly laid concrete path, he calmly walked up to the front door letterbox to insert the mail, having no idea that it was not set and leaving his footprints on the entire length of the path. If you were lucky enough to receive a postcard, he would stand and read it to you before handing it over.

The life wasn't idyllic, very hard, labour intensive work and times of stress. Frud's mother Lucy was diagnosed with breast cancer, the removal of her breast was undertaken by the local doctor on the kitchen table! September

1936 Last night Anne got her teeth, 38 years old! Presumably her false teeth, very young to lose all of her teeth but then dentistry was rudimentary and in its infancy.

Some of Frud's Diary entries, in his own words!

Xmas Day 1923 went to see football match, Belton 3 Burgh Castle 5. 25th December 1924 Father and I went and had look at football between married and single. 26th December 1924 in afternoon had a look at Burgh and Belton playing football, it was a draw. 17th January 1926 Jewson's played football with Belton, goals 3 -1.

Belton Football team circa 1930s, Bertie (Jellicoe) Saul back row 4ᵗʰ from left

23rd Jan 1924 Gramophone came up at night. 7th June 1925, Knights come up in his motor and took Herbert, Dudley and I for a ride round. 24th October 1925 I went to Norwich with Herbert Knights in his motorcar. 7th November 1925 Tom and Kenny come up after us in motor car, we went over to Slater's then to Lowestoft where Tom was married, then back to Slater's. We were drove home in the early morning in a car, Kenny slept at mine. 18th December 1925 went to children's concert down at the Institute last night and tonight. 17th January 1926 sharp frost, skating on the pond. 6th May 1935 Jubilee day, celebrating the Silver Jubilee of King George V, all the children of the village up to the age of 15 had a mug. 10th June 19?? Father, Harry and I drove in motor car to Ellough marsh farm. 10th September 1930 Yesterday I went for an aeroplane flight for the first time.

Frud's diary recorded numerous tragedies in Belton as listed below:

July 1929 Harry Skipper and Eric Hall drowned in the river. Sep 1929 Lion Balls strangled himself. March 1930 Ernest Varnell buried, 32 years old. Jan 1930 the young Wilstead found on the line near Bell Lane Bridge with his head off. April 1930 at night, coming home from the fair George Barber was killed. May 1930 George Barber buried, a Buff funeral, (The Royal Antediluvian Order of Buffaloes) the first in Belton. He was 47 years old. Canham took the wreaths on the lorry with the chestnut mare. Nov 1931 Billy Meale died in hospital aged 44 years. April 1932 Sam Beare shot himself 59 years old. His father also committed suicide. May 1932 Sailor Jessop was buried, 32 years old. Jan 1933 Kelly Coleman buried, 28 years old. Oct 1935 George Punchard buried 22 years old. March 1936 Mrs. Harry Beare died very suddenly. Dec 1936 Edgar Bland shot himself, 58 years old. January 1937 George Searby was buried yesterday, 21 years old. April 1937 Harry Payne's little girl died. Jan 1938 Yesterday Tommy Castle from Burgh Castle was drowned in the river near Porter's timber yard. June 1942 at night time Sam Skipper was killed by a motor car at the bottom of Bland's Hill. The car driver was a Mr. Hingly, he was excluded from blame. Harry Brain (gamekeeper) was shot and taken to Lowestoft hospital. Ivan Gray tried to commit suicide. Matthew Mann shot himself.

The number of male suicides is surprising and many people died before their time. Some of these deaths were as a result of accidents, Health and Safety was practically non-existent compared to today. Some no doubt were due to infectious diseases, e.g. influenza, pneumonia, tuberculosis, scarlet fever, smallpox and diphtheria, most of which today are curable due to advances in medicine, in the early 20th century they were not. This was also before the introduction of immunisation. Suicide rates increased in the 1930s, coinciding with the Great Depression. The 'breadwinner' i.e. the husband would have felt inadequate if he couldn't provide for his family, this would have undoubtedly lead to anxiety and depression and ultimately an inability to cope, resulting in suicide. One man who committed suicide lost an arm when working with a traction engine / threshing machine, machinery had no guards at this time. He couldn't provide for his family and subsequently feeling desolate ended his life. There was no state welfare as such at this time. Another diary entry states that in 1935, 22 year old Jack Pleasants had his leg amputated at Norwich hospital.

The diary also included some amusing entries: *July 1933 a cow fell down Walter Sharman's well. July 1936 Rev. Jones went to Lowestoft courts for being drunk in charge of a motor car, got clear. November 1925 Herbert and I went to Yarmouth County Court, I was fined 30s for hitting Beare and Mannell as they*

were cutting my privet hedge. 1935 P.
Beare fell off his horse. Derek and John
took the rats down to Becks, 2d each.
(Becks was the village butcher!)

There were also other interesting entries:
Lound mill was working in the 1930s
grinding cereals. St Johns Farm, an
ancient farm house, barn, outbuildings
and 23 acres of land sold in 1932 for
£690.

Many growers today make costly machinery
purchases collaboratively and then share the use
of the machine. Collaboration between growers
was however being undertaken in the 1930s e.g.
Got Searby's drag rake and done the
Glebe, Browston and Turnpike fields.
Walter putting lime out on the Big field
with Searby's drill. Herbert drilling
wheat for F. Searby. Roger getting a
load of old sprouts from Searby's. Cut
Searby's oats in the corner field. Got a
load of cinders and load of cabbages for
the cows from Searby's. Henry carted

some sugar beet tops from Searby's. I went after two loads of sprout trimmings for the cows from Searby's. Father bought hay from Searby, £15. Roger got load of cabbages from Searby's. Henry went with Searby's lorry and ours after two loads of beet pulp at Cantley.

World War Two

As in World War One, once again food production was of vital, and arguably even more, importance. Britain imported 70% of its food; this required 20 million tons of shipping a year. 50% of meat was imported, 70% of cheese and sugar, 80% of fruits, 70% of cereals and fats, 91% of butter. Of this, $^1/_6$ of meat imports, ¼ of butter imports and ½ of cheese imports came from New Zealand alone, by ship. German U-boats severely disrupted allied merchant convoys in the Atlantic attempting to bring much needed food supplies to the UK. The Axis powers hoped to starve the British population into submission, by cutting off those food supply lines.

The Ministry of Food regulated how grocers got the food that they sold to their customers. They were told to get their supplies from the nearest wholesaler or maker of the item, in order to reduce distribution costs and save petrol, rather than shopping around and ordering in items from around the country. Once again, this increased demand for locally sourced food benefitted the market garden and farm. Just prior to the war farmers had been going through terrible times and they were really on their uppers. Prices improved tremendously as the war produced much better financial returns for all the farmers.

Essentially there was just one buyer, the Government, who would set the prices for produce. All produce had to be sent to a 'pool' for fair distribution. Growers were also directed how to glean maximum productivity from their land, every scrap of land had to be utilised to grow food. Grassland for livestock was inefficient as this could only feed a few people per acre in comparison with arable land. Market control by Government inevitably resulted in the 'creative trading' of produce with eyebrow raising cucumbers down a man's trousers. Even

Lord Somerleyton would arrive at Pansy Villa for a cucumber and a pound of tomatoes, probably bartered for a pheasant.

During WW2 there was still a demand for cut flowers. Frud therefore decided to leave a patch of land in the middle of a cereal field where he grew cut flowers to satisfy this demand. This concealed the growing of cut flowers from the Ministry of Food inspectors!

While ploughing with horses a German fighter plane appeared, rather than return home with bullets in his guns he decided to fire them at Frud. The horses bolted, Frud hung on tight to the reins and was dragged the entire length of the field only stopped by a barbed wire fence. The poor horses survived this traumatic experience but one was severely lacerated by the barbed wire with a huge L shaped cut across the chest, which Frud had to sew up.

The Botwrights during the war benefitted from their own vegetables, milk, butter, cheese, chickens, eggs and they kept pigs which were killed and preserved using salt. People in rural villages could also forage for wild fruits such as blackberries and even hawthorn berries, they could also shoot rabbits, ducks, geese and some even poached his lordship's pheasants to provide food for the table, many rural folk owned a shotgun. The acquisition of food was much easier in the countryside, less so in the towns and cities, the people had a hard time acquiring food with meagre rations.

Remarkably, work and life appeared to have carried on regardless of the issues brought about by the war, no doubt enhanced by the tenacious British bulldog spirit. The workers on the farm and market garden are now working long hours, dawn until dusk, finishing at 9pm, daylight permitting.

Frud's diary entries during WW2, in his own words!
12th Jan 1940 Tonight the Institute was closed down so as the soldiers can have it for to train in and have their meals.
15th Jan 1940 The soldiers come to Belton and were billeted in different

houses, they have their meals in the Institute.

24th Jan 1940 Anne, Marjorie, Peter and Bertie went to whist drive tonight for to send the service men a parcel. There is a lot of soldiers billeted in Belton now.

30th Jan 1940 Flossie Smiths husband Rumsby was drowned in a small boat after the Germans had bombed the lightship he was on. Rumsby was buried at Bungay.

29th May 1940 The Paras went on duty this week.

11th July 1940 in the morning, the Germans bombed Southtown Road.

24th January 1941 Threshing barley in the Church field, it was foggy and as we were threshing a German bomber flew past, he dropped his bombs against the Yarmouth destructor, no doubt a near go for us, that he did not machine gun us.

3rd February 1941 Siren have been several times today.

5th February 1941 Bombs dropped at Gypsy Green, Bradwell.

3rd March 1941 I went to Yarmouth, had a look at where the bombs dropped.

23rd March 1941 Church parade all over the empire.

5th April 1941 Harry Payne registered today.

7th April 1941 I was stopped by two special constables because my side lights were too big. I went to court for my lorry lights, fined £1 7s. On Saturday PC Button asked me to do fire watching in the village, he have got 60 watchers from the station up to mine.

8th April 1941 Big raid on Yarmouth last night, lot of damage done.

11th April 1941 Lot of damage done at Yarmouth last night.

18th April 1941 Last night Anne and Ronnie Todd were killed on Cobholm Island by a bomb.

23rd June 1941 there were 70 to 100 fire bombs fell on the Glebe land in Belton.

5th July 1941 Herbert Bond registered today.

9th Jan 1942 Henry and I done fire watching all night at the station.

Jan 1942 Henry and I went to Walter Jermy's for to see about a permit to grow cues.

16th Feb 1942 Went to Yarmouth, could not get any wood. A barrage balloon come down on the marshes, PC Button and Alan Sharman come after it after Jellico had reported it.

17th Feb 1942 Peter (Frud's son who had joined the navy) come home on leave this morning.

24th Feb 1942 Peter went to Portsmouth Naval Base, he has had seven days leave, his first.

15th March 1942 Home guard and soldiers had a sham fight in Belton.

19th April 1942 Peter went away.

30th April 1942 Most of the men in Belton received papers to join the Home Guard. Norwich was bombed again last night, the place look alight.

Initially bombed in the summer of 1940, Norwich was subsequently not attacked until April and May 1942 as part of the so-called Baedeker raids, in which targets were chosen for their cultural and historical value and not as a strategic or military target. The most devastating of these attacks occurred on the evening of 27 April 1942 and continued again on 29 April. There were further attacks in May and a heavy bombardment on 26 and 27 June in which Norwich Cathedral was damaged. Norwich Castle, the City Hall and the Guildhall escaped while many residential streets were destroyed. Norwich suffered extensive bomb damage during the Second World War, affecting large parts of the old city centre and Victorian terrace housing around the centre. Industry and rail infrastructure also suffered. The heaviest raids occurred on the nights of 27/28 and 29/30 April 1942; as part of the Baedeker raids; attacks on Bath, Canterbury, Norwich, Exeter, and York using Baedeker's series of tourist guides to the British Isles. Norwich became one of the targets of the so-called "Baedeker Blitz", which took place in retaliation for the bombing of Lübeck by the RAF earlier that year.

10th May 1942 Henry joined the Home Guard.

17th May 1942 Roger joined the Home Guard.

22nd May 1942 I went to Beccles after some pigs. On my way, the other side of Toft Lion I was run into by an RAF lorry loaded with brick rubble, he did not stop till I caught up with him on the Bungay road.

28th May 1942 Last night all went to Home Guard except Herbert and me. Have not heard from Peter for nearly a week.

31st May 1942 Big raid over Germany last night, over 1,000 planes used.

30/31 May 1942 attack on Cologne was the first 1,000 bomber raid.

14th June 1942 Peter's girl (Winnie) come over.

22nd June 1942 Anne had a letter from Peter after about six weeks. The Fall of Tobruk, captured by the Germans.

24th June 1942 War look bad in North Africa.

25th June 1942 *this morning there was a huge fire in Yarmouth, the parish church burned out by a Jerry aeroplane when some bombs were dropped.*

7th July 1942 *renewed my tomato licence, retail and wholesale. Roger and Bertie carting cinders from the bombed destructor.*

24th July 1942 *I went to Pordage's at Yarmouth with tomatoes for the pool at night time.* The Ministry of Food became the sole buyer and importer of food and regulated prices, guaranteeing farmers' prices and markets for their produce. The Combined Food Board was set up in 1942 to pool food resources.

8th August 1942 *Very short of petrol just now. Rationed*

8th Sep 1942 *I went down to the Rectory at night time to see about something for the Service funds.*

15th Sep 1942 *Mr. Adcock the fuel officer come over.*

4th Oct 1942 *Home Guard marches about Belton.*

5th Oct 1942 went down the Rectory at night time to see about the Service fund.

29th Oct 1942 Sent Chrysanths away, it seem as if it will be the last we shall send away till the war is over.

9th Nov 1942 Peter came home.

12th Nov 1942 Mother and Peter went over to Haddiscoe.

14th Nov 1942 Peter went away, he was called back.

25th Nov 1942 Hazel (Frud's niece) went away this morning.

30th Dec 1942 Reggie Botwright come to live in Arthur Moy's bungalow.

3rd Jan 1943 Hazel come home for the first time.

18th Jan 1943 Jack (Frud's nephew) went away to be a sailor.

1st Feb 1943 Dennis Sharman went away today. (He died in the war)

21st Feb 1943 This week the government took all the iron rails and gates all round Belton. (The country badly needed metal for munitions, so requisitioned and removed iron rails and gates under Regulation 50 of the Defence (General) Regulations, 1939)

2nd April 1943 Jack went to Chatham Royal Naval Barracks.

5th May 1943 Father, E. Morse and I went to a tomato meeting at Hopton Hart.

7th May 1943 several bombs dropped on Yarmouth this morning, many people killed.

9th May 1943 Went to church, Wings for Victory week.

10th May 1943 had a telegram from Peter.

11th May 1943 This morning a German bomb killed poor Allan Powley.

16th May 1943 Anne, Peter and I went over to Winterton and had a look at the houses which were bombed.

20th May 1943 have now planted about 35 thousand outside tomato plants. Have sent the first Pyrethrums away to Newcastle today and the railway will not take any more there.

11th June 1943 Gathered and took tomatoes to the pool for the first time this year.

23rd June 1943 sent a lot of cabbages to Brentford. Took tomatoes into the pool.

2nd July 1943 Gathering and packing tomatoes, took them to the pool at Yarmouth.

23rd July 1943 Peter is 21 today. Jack Saul went away today.

24th Sep 1943 some of the men have been gathering tomatoes all day, have got between six and seven hundred boxes.

18th Oct 1943 Packing tomatoes all day, Peter and I took them to Vauxhall station ready to go to Worksop, no empties about. Been asked to grow so many tomatoes run out of boxes to put them in.

24th Oct 1943 Peter went away to Hull this morning.

7th Nov 1943 Peter is at Portsmouth.

2nd Dec 1943 Peter come home on Embarkation leave, he thinks he is to go to New Jersey.

8th Dec 1943 Peter went away this morning.

13th Dec 1943 Peter left the Portsmouth barracks for America.

31st Dec 1943 it looks as if Peter got to USA on the 22nd December.

2nd Feb 1944 have had a letter from Peter, he seems to have left New York and is on HMS Thornborough.

6th June 1944 Early this morning the Second Front (D-Day) began, a day in our lives to remember.

7th - 18th June Going well on the Second Front.

For whatever reason the daily diary entries petered out during 1944 and finally ceased altogether.

Belton Parishioners who lost their lives in WW2:
Thomas C. Arscott, Charles A. T. Burfoot, Alan A. Holmes, Cyril F. Meale, Reginald J. Pleasance, Herbert Rumsby, Dennis R. Sharman, Edgar A. Sharman, George A. F. Sharman and Frank Simpson.

Burgh Castle Parishioners who lost their lives in WW2:

Percy William Godtbill, William Redvers Rolfe, Charles Ambrose Mace, Harry Leonard Perfect, Nelson Frederick Basil Sayer, George Henry Wright,, Arthur James Davies and Clive Granville Harvey.

Peter's Navy Service

Peter worked on the farm and milk round but was unenthused by this life, he was keen to get away from his destiny of working for his imperious grandfather of whom he had a considerable disregard, punching him in the stomach when he was a boy and uttering the words "you fat ole bugger", so he enrolled in the Navy, possibly before he was legally entitled to so do.

Leading Seaman Peter Botwright DSM

Peter's naval service took him to Scotland, France, Gibraltar, Malta, Egypt, The Azores, Gambia, Nigeria, Senegal, Ghana, Sierra Leone, South Africa, Brazil, Trinidad and the USA.

Peter served on numerous ships including: HMS Trouncer (D85) Ruler-class escort aircraft carrier. HMS Woodruff (K53) Flower-class corvette. HMS Thornborough (K574) a British Captain-class frigate. HMS Campbeltown (I42) a Town-class destroyer.

As an obsolescent destroyer, launched in 1919, Campbeltown was considered to be expendable and was selected to be the ram-ship used in the St. Nazaire Raid (Operation Chariot) in 1942. One of the most daring and audacious operations of the Second World War, known as "The Greatest Raid of All", Operation Chariot was an attack on the dry docks at St Nazaire in German-occupied France, to stop German battleships such as Bismark and Tirpitz from accessing maintenance facilities while operating in the Atlantic Ocean.

HMS Campbeltown having rammed the dry dock at St. Nazaire loaded with explosives.

The Thornborough, Normandy Landings and beyond

HMS Thornborough, a Captain-class frigate, was built in the USA at Bethlehem Hingham Shipyard, Massachusetts, launched on the 13th November 1943. Captain-class frigates acted in the roles of convoy escorts, anti-submarine warfare vessels, coastal forces control frigates and headquarters ships for the Normandy landings. Frud's diary notes that Peter travelled to the USA leaving Portsmouth on 13/12/43 arriving in the USA on 22/12/43 to collect this newly built ship on which he was then based. Battle Honours for HMS Thornborough include: Atlantic, English Channel, Normandy 6th June 1944, North Foreland and North Sea.

HMS Thornborough

Royal Navy official photographer
(https://commons.wikimedia.org/wiki/File:HMS_Thornborough_WWII_IWM_A_2564 0.jpg), „HMS Thornborough WWII IWM A 25640", marked as public domain, more details on Wikimedia Commons: https://commons.wikimedia.org/wiki/Template:PD-UKGov

Leading Seaman Peter Botwright PJX314593, served in the Royal Navy, receiving the Distinguished Service Medal (DSM) during the Normandy D-Day Landings, Operation Neptune which formed part of Operation Overlord. Peter was serving on HMS Thornborough which was off Sword Beach. The D.S.M. was awarded to Peter Botwright for bravery and resourcefulness on active service at sea and setting an example of bravery and resource under fire.

This honour was for jumping into the sea to rescue his fellow compatriots, even though he could not swim. Peter simply tied a rope, attached to the ship, around his midriff.

October 1944.

Sir,

I am commanded by My Lords Commissioners of the Admiralty to inform you that they have learned with great pleasure that, on the advice of the First Lord, the King has been graciously pleased to award you the Distinguished Service Medal for courage, skill and devotion to duty shown in H.M.S. THORNBOROUGH in operations in connection with the invasion of Normandy.

This Award was published in the London Gazette Supplement of 24th October 1944.

I am, Sir,

Your obedient Servant,

Leading Seaman Peter Botwright, D.S.M.

DSM Award letter

Leading - Seaman Peter Botwright, R.N., the 22-year-old son of Mr. and Mrs. F. Botwright, of Pansy Villa, Belton, who has been awarded the D.S.M. for distinguished services on one of H.M. ships during the invasion of Normandy.

After D-Day, for the next few months, German ships in French ports were attempting to break out of the ports of Northern France under cover of darkness. HMS Thornborough was involved in preventing this exodus of German naval ships. Before dawn on the 24/8/1944 Thornborough along with other allied ships intercepted and sunk a north-bound enemy convoy consisting of six gun coasters and an R-boat off Cap d'Antifer.

Fire on board the SS Empire Patrol.

Peter was involved in various rescues at sea, most memorably, the SS Empire Patrol in the Mediterranean Sea. Peter, aboard HMS Trouncer, was involved in the evacuation of about five hundred Dodecanese Greek refugees from the SS Empire Patrol on the 29th of September 1945. Most of the ship was on fire, many had jumped into the water and drifted far and wide. Some were in boats, on rafts, and some with only lifejackets, 300 remained on board, but as the fire spread, with diminishing safe space. The main problem was that the Trouncer towered above the Empire Patrol with overhanging flight decks and no deck to transfer the refugees anywhere near the waterline.

Ruler-class escort carrier HMS Trouncer (D85)

The following page:
Survivors from the SS Empire Patrol board the Trouncer 1 October 1945, 38 miles off Port Said

Many family members served their country including Frud who served in the navy in WW1, Peter served in the navy in WW2, Jack Saul, Frud's nephew, also served in the navy in WW2, Hazel Bond, Frud's niece served in the WRENs (Women's Royal Naval Service) and Frud, his brother Roger and his brother-in-law's Henry Saul and Herbert Bond enlisted in the Home Guard during WW2.

Belton & Burgh Castle Home Guard

*Davy Beare of Browston, in his Home Guard
uniform, ready for action!*

Planned resistance: Auxiliary Units.

Pte Reginald John Botwright, a very distant relative of Frud, who, coincidentally, lived at the top of Lawns Lane, Belton was a member of the local Auxiliary Unit. This was a **highly secret,** specially trained, resistance force, created in WW2, to help combat an invasion. Men were trained in guerrilla warfare, assassination, unarmed combat, demolition and sabotage. Their role was to attack invading forces from behind their own lines. Aircraft, fuel dumps, railway lines and depots were high on the list of targets, as were senior German officers. Men were recruited from farmers, landowners, gamekeepers, poachers and the Home Guard, have a thorough knowledge of the locality and were able to live off the land. If invasion came they would relocate to a concealed underground bunker, with a camouflaged entrance and emergency escape tunnel. These men had an expected lifespan of 14 days if an invasion came.

Reginald Botwright had a Ladies and Gentlemen's hairdressers behind the ABC cinema just off the market place in Great Yarmouth and lived in Belton. Reginald

Botwright lost his brother Corporal 43086 Herbert Jeffrey Botwright, 5th Division of the 1st Battalion, Norfolk Regiment. Killed in action 25th September 1916 aged 27. Son of Herbert and Evelyn Botwright of 55 Market Place, Great Yarmouth. Born in Great Yarmouth and enlisted in Norwich. Herbert is buried in the Guards Cemetery, Lesboeufs, Departement de la Somme, Picardie, France. The little village of Lesboeufs, on the Somme, was attacked by the Guards Division on 15th September 1916 and captured by them on the 25th. He therefore tragically died on the day that the battle was won.

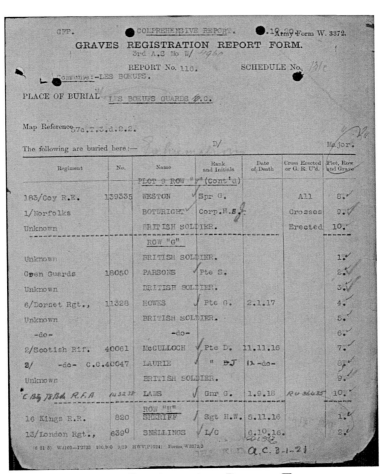

GRAVES REGISTRATION REPORT FORM.

3rd A.C No W/ 4960

REPORT No. 116.   SCHEDULE No. 13/c

PLACE OF BURIAL LES BOEUFS GUARDS M.C.

Map Reference 57c.T.3.d.2.2.

The following are buried here:—   D/   Major.

Regiment	No.	Name	Rank and Initials	Date of Death	Cross Erected or G. R. U'd.	Plot, Row and Grave
		PLOT 9 ROW "F" (Cont'd)				
183/Coy R.E.	139335	WESTON	Spr G.		All	8.
1/Norfolks		BOTWRIGHT	Corp.H.E.		Crosses	9.
Unknown		BRITISH SOLDIER.			Erected	10.
		ROW "G"				
Unknown		BRITISH SOLDIER.				1.
Coen Guards	18050	PARSONS	Pte S.			2.
Unknown		BRITISH SOLDIER.				3.
6/Dorset Rgt.,	11328	HOWES	Pte G.	2.1.17		4.
Unknown		BRITISH SOLDIER.				5.
-do-		-do-				6.
2/Scottish Rif.	40061	McCULLOCH	Pte D.	11.11.16		7.
2/ -do- C.C.40047		LAURIE	" D.J.	12.-do-		8.
Unknown		BRITISH SOLDIER.				9.
C 12g 78/Bd. R.F.A	143238	LAWS	Gnr G.	1.9.18	R U 36635	10.
		ROW "H"				
16 Kings R.R.	820	SHERIFF	Sgt H.W.	5.11.16		1.
13/London Rgt.,	6390	SNELLINGS	L/C	6.10.16.		2.

(6 31 5) WJ100—T2725 100,000 9/19 HWV(P1024) Forms W3372,3

KRD Q.C. 3-1-21

Graves Registration Report Form

Imperial War Graves Commission.

COMPREHENSIVE REPORT (A) OF HEADSTONE INSCRIPTIONS
to this report is attached

COMPREHENSIVE REPORT (B) HEADSTONE TEXTS
(those headstones to be inscribed with texts are underlined)

and

TWO STANDARD LAYOUTS (the layouts to be used are quoted on the badge design).

Schedule "A" Page ___ 17

Name of Cemetery.

GUARDS CEM. LES BOEUFS "D"

To be stencilled on foot of
headstones below ground level
abbreviated thus :—

GDS.C.L/BOE.

Badge Design No. and Layout No.	1st Line.	2nd Line.	3rd Line.	4th Line.	Age.	Centre of Stone.	To be stencilled on foot of Headstones below ground level.	
	Number and Rank.	Initials, NAME and Honours.	Regiment.	Date of Death. In any instance where the entry "JOINT" appears in Col. 6, the Age will be omitted from the Headstone and the Date of Death entered laterally.		Bdg. Emb.	Plot P. Row R. Grave G.	No. of Stone.
(1)	(2)	(3)	(4)	(5)	(6)	(7)	(8)	(9)
1029/1G		UNKNOWN BRITISH SOLDIER (FOR PARTICULARS OF LAYOUT INSC. ETC. SEE SCHED. G/H)					9 S S	1741
LAYOUT 1H		UNKNOWN BRITISH SOLDIER (FOR PARTICULARS OF LAYOUT INSC. ETC. SEE SCHED. G/H)					9 S 6	1742
Layout 1H		Unknown British Soldier (		ols)			9 S 7	1743
LAYOUT 1H		UNKNOWN BRITISH SOLDIER (FOR PARTICULARS OF LAYOUT INSC. ETC. SEE SCHED. G/H)					9 S S	1744
1002/1D	16451 GUARDSMAN	A. FORD	GRENADIER GUARDS	21ST SEPTEMBER 1916	AGE 26	CROSS	9 S 9	1745
Layout 1H Unknown British Soldier		(for particulars of layout see sched left)					9 S 10	1746
1186/1G 1066		UNKNOWN BRITISH SOLDIER (FOR PARTICULARS OF LAYOUT INSC. ETC. SEE SCHED. G/H)					9 P 1	1747
1106/1C	73050 PRIVATE	H. J. JONES	WELCH REGIMENT	30TH AUGUST 1916	AGE 19	CROSS	9 P 2	1748
1106/2D	73256 GUNNER	A. W. NEWMAN	ROYAL GARRISON ARTILLERY	2ND OCTOBER 1916	AGE 19	CROSS	9 P 3	1749
1106/2A	34544 SERJEANT	J. PEAT, MM.	ROYAL GARRISON ARTILLERY	17TH JANUARY 1917	AGE 22	CROSS	9 P 4	1750
LAYOUT 1H		UNKNOWN BRITISH SOLDIER (FOR PARTICULARS OF LAYOUT INSC. ETC. SEE SCHED. G/H)					9 P 5	1751
1186/2A	31805 SERJEANT	G. E. TILYARD	ROYAL GARRISON ARTILLERY	17TH JANUARY 1917	AGE 22	CROSS	9 P 6	1752
LAYOUT 1H		UNKNOWN BRITISH SOLDIER (FOR PARTICULARS OF LAYOUT INSC. ETC. SEE SCHED. G/H)					9 P 7	1753
1190/1A	139338 SAPPER	G. WESTON	ROYAL ENGINEERS	1ST SEPTEMBER 1918	NONE	CROSS	9 P 8	1754
1042/1A	43066 CORPORAL	J. BOTWRIGHT	NORFOLK REGIMENT	26TH SEPTEMBER 1916	NONE	CROSS	9 P 9	1755

To X Gr. 64 - 1746

Stone no. 1743 to X Group 90

*A special _____ is provided
*For use with this headstone)

Headstone report

1945 to 1952 dissolution

When Fred snr was in his eighties he fell asleep sitting in the chair in front of the open fire, he fell out of the chair knocking himself out on the fire grate. Being unconscious, he lay there for some time before help arrived to remove him from the fire, by which time he had burnt the entire side of his face.

Fred snr died in 1948, soon after, Frud decided that he wanted away from the resultant three-way partnership but his two brothers were not keen for this to happen. Frud therefore instigated the dissolution of Botwright bros. The farm, houses and market garden were auctioned on the 17th June 1953. The two remaining brothers Roger and Harry purchased the lot. With his proceeds from the sale Frud purchased Hornerthorpe, a market garden in Burgh Castle.

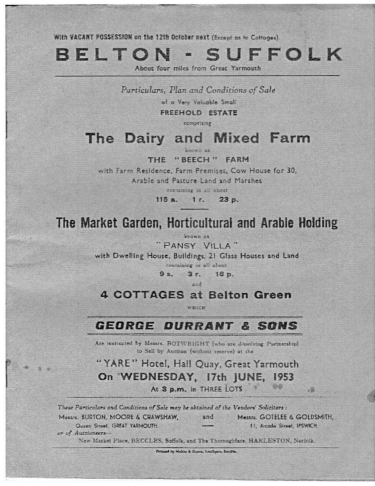

With VACANT POSSESSION on the 12th October next (Except as to Cottages).

BELTON - SUFFOLK

About four miles from Great Yarmouth

Particulars, Plan and Conditions of Sale

of a Very Valuable Small

FREEHOLD ESTATE

comprising

The Dairy and Mixed Farm

known as

THE "BEECH" FARM

with Farm Residence, Farm Premises, Cow House for 30,
Arable and Pasture Land and Marshes

containing in all about

115 a.   1 r.   23 p.

The Market Garden, Horticultural and Arable Holding

known as

"PANSY VILLA"

with Dwelling House, Buildings, 21 Glass Houses and Land

containing in all about

9 a.   3 r.   16 p.

and

4 COTTAGES at Belton Green

WHICH

GEORGE DURRANT & SONS

Are instructed by Messrs. BOTWRIGHT (who are dissolving Partnership)
to Sell by Auction (without reserve) at the

"YARE" Hotel, Hall Quay, Great Yarmouth

On WEDNESDAY, 17th JUNE, 1953

At 3 p.m. In THREE LOTS

These Particulars and Conditions of Sale may be obtained of the Vendors' Solicitors :

Messrs. BURTON, MOORE & CRAWSHAW,   and   Messrs. GOTELEE & GOLDSMITH,
Queen Street, GREAT YARMOUTH.   ——   11, Arcade Street, IPSWICH.
or of Auctioneers—
New Market Place, BECCLES, Suffolk, and The Thoroughfare, HARLESTON, Norfolk.

Printed by Nobbs & Cross, Southgate, Beccles.

*Auction catalogue of Beech Farm, Pansy Villa
and cottages, giving some indication of the
amenities of dwellings at this time.*

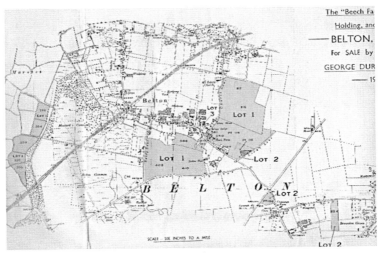

SCALE . SIX INCHES TO A MILE

Auction catalogue map

"The Beech Farm" comprising an attractive brick
and slated RESIDENTIAL FARM HOUSE
pleasantly situated with South aspect, containing
Sunken Cellarage; Porch with coloured glass
windows and tiled floor; Entrance Hall; Drawing
Room, about 14ft x 13ft 10ins, with boarded
floor, register stove, marble mantelpiece, E.L.
point and partly glazed door to Garden; Dining
Room, about 14ft x 14ft, with boarded floor,
register stove, marble mantelpiece, small wall
cupboard, E.L. point and power plug; Back Hall
and Lobby with cupboard under stairs, E.L.
point; Dairy with brick floor, shelving and E.L.
point; Kitchen, about 14ft x 13ft, with brick floor,

4ft. cooking range with boiler, recess cupboards, E.L. point and wall plug; Scullery with tiled floor, glazed sink with water tap from supply tank, 2ft 6in cooking range, Dutch oven, E.L. point and wall plug; Pantry with brick floor and shelving; Lean-to brick and slated Store Room with part cement and part tiled floor and door to yard; well-lighted Staircase and Landing with E.L. point and wall plug; Five good Bedrooms (four with stoves and all with E.L. points); Two Box or Store Rooms; Lean-to brick, boarded and glazed Covered Way with concrete floor to Back Entrance; Back Yard with concrete pathway and brick and slated Store Shed; lean-to asbestos Milk House, with E.L. point and water tap; Pump from well and water tap with timber and corrugated iron cover; boarded and corrugated iron Pump House with Lister Electric Pump, raising good spring water from Well to 500-gallon Supply Tank outside and a corrugated iron extension over copper and furnace; Lean-to boarded Churn-cooling House, with concrete floor, part concrete walls and water tap; Lean-to brick and tiled Earth Closet; Detached boarded and corrugated iron-roofed Workshop, with bench, vice, clamp, cupboards, nests of drawers and E.L. point; also boarded and corrugated iron Store House on wheels; E.L. point on House.

SET OF FARM BUILDINGS consisting of brick and thatched Cart Horse Stable for six, with E.L. point and Loft over; Brick and tiled lean-to Harness House with E.L. point and Chaff Bin; Brick and tiled Nag Stable with E.L. point and Gig House with part concrete and part brick floor, E.L. point and Granary over approached by outside steps. Adjoining in rear are two boarded and tiled Loose Boxes on brick pinion, with one E.L, point and mangers; Range of Six brick, timber and tiled Loose Boxes and Two-bay Hovel with Spacious Yards (each Box having Mangers and two E.L. points for all); Large brick and thatched Barn with part concrete and part boarded floor, three E.L. points, 6-h.p. Fairbanks paraffin Engine, Loft over part and brick and tiled Porch; Cow House for 30, with concrete floor, wood mangers, stalls, feeding passage and five E.L. points; Cow and Cattle Yards with shedding; Two brick and tiled Pig Sties with concrete floors and courts; Range of brick and tiled Premises, comprising Store House, Coal House, Wood House and Meal House; Detached Four-bay brick, timber and thatched Cart Shed and Loose Box; Asbestos and tiled Tractor Shed with cement floor; Large corrugated iron Implement Shed; Corrugated iron Oil Shed with cement floor; Sunken 300-

gallon Petrol Tank with Pump; 250.gallon
T.V.O. Tank with asbestos cover on wood stand;
Stack Yard with iron fencing, and Enclosures of
Highly Productive MIXED SOIL ARABLE
LAND mainly abutting upon public roads and in
a high state of cultivation, much of it being well-
adapted for Building or Market Gardening on an
extensive scale; Old Pasture Land and FIVE
GRAZING MARSHES approached from Station
Road by Sandy Lane and Marsh Lane, with
corrugated iron Milking Shed for 10 Cows, and
Cake House adjoining, the whole containing by
Ordnance Survey and admeasurement 115 a. 1 r.
23 p.

MARKET GARDEN, HORTICULTURAL
AND ARABLE HOLDING "Pansy Villa" most
conveniently situate adjoining Lot 1 and Lawn's
Lane, one enclosure adjoining the main Beccles-
Great Yarmouth Road and another adjoining
Cherry Lane, Browston, and known as "Pansy
Villa" comprising a brick, part flint and tiled
DWELLING HOUSE containing Front Entrance
and Lobby; Two Front Sitting Rooms, about 11ft
6ins x 10ft 9ins and 10ft 9ins x 10ft 6ins, with
boarded floors, tiled surround stoves and marble
mantels, E.L. points and one with cupboards;
Living Room about 12ft x 9ft, with modern tiled

stove, boarded floor, E.L. point and wall plug; Pantry with shelving; Staircase and small Landing with wall plug; Four Bedrooms (two with stoves, one with wardrobe cupboard and three with E.L. points); a glazed, covered way with concrete floor and two outside entrances at the back of the House gives access to the Living Room, also to attached lean-to brick and tiled Kitchen, about 20ft 6ins x 12ft, with concrete floor, matchboard lined ceiling, 2ft 6in cooking range, glazed, sink with soft water pump over, copper, E.L. point, wall plug and cooker point; Lean-to Conservatory about 18ft x 12ft, with concrete floor, s.c. stove and shelving at West end of house. Pump of drinking water by back entrance; Brick and tiled Earth closet. Mains Electricity is installed to House and there are three E.L. points outside.

EXTENSIVE BUILDINGS consisting of a capital two-span matchboard and corrugated iron Packing Store (one span about 28ft 6ins x 26ft and the other about 28ft 6ins x 21ft 6ins) each with concrete floors, double doors to roadway and back entrance, communicating door and small partitioned Office; well-lighted timber and corrugated span-roof Packing Shed with concrete floor, about 29ft x 15ft, with double entrance doors and double door; Boarded and corrugated iron Garage or Gig House, with double entrance doors and lean-to Workshop with concrete floor and bench with vice affixed; Corrugated iron span-roof Coal Store; Range of boarded, corrugated iron and tiled roof Stabling with concrete floor, attached corrugated iron Store Shed with double doors and small lean-to Store Shed; Detached timber and corrugated iron Cart Shed with concrete floor; two boarded and tiled Pig Sties with courts and Meal Store adjoining; Asbestos and corrugated iron Pumping Shed with concrete floor, deep cylinder Well, 1½-h.p. Lister petrol Engine and Pump; Large brick Reservoir for water supply, and a Valuable Range of 21SPAN GLASS HOUSES nineteen heated by six boilers and furnaces, two un-heated, and all with piped water supply, covering an area of approximately 22,559 Square Feet. MARKET GARDEN, HORTICULTURAL AND ARABLE LAND abutting upon the High Road and containing 9 a. 3 r. 16 p.

The initials a (acre) r (rood) p (perch) refers to Imperial measurements of area used at this time to measure land.

193

30¼ square yards	1 perch
40 perches	1 rood
4 roods	1 acre

1952 to 1964 Hornerthorpe

Once the dissolution of the Botwright Bros partnership had been completed, Frud and Anne purchased a smallholding in Burgh Castle from Ernie Green called Hornerthorpe. This consisted of a large three bedroom house, with an enclosed concrete yard, wash house with sink, tap and copper, coal house, Elsan Closet (chemical toilet), a small front garden and a walled vegetable garden. Water was pumped from a well by a recently installed automatic deep well electric pump to a pressure tank in the barn and from there to the washhouse.

One of the first things he undertook was to build a significant area of glass houses. He was able to utilise his 50 years of experience, continuing to grow tomatoes and cucumbers in the glass houses, numerous varieties of cut flowers and a selection of vegetables, these were mainly sold on the market stall in Great Yarmouth. He continued to send flowers to various parts of the country despite the fact that the railway that ran through the village was on the verge of closing. It's quite amazing that at the age of 60, an age when others might consider retiring, Frud started and established a new business.

It is believed that Hornerthorpe was built from the local brick made at Burgh Castle Brick and Cement Works, less than ½ mile away, which opened in 1859 and closed in 1912. The brickworks covered a vast area of around 50 acres from the Roman Walls to the Belton/Burgh Parish boundary. It can be no coincidence that its name relates to a director of the brick works namely Joseph Horner. His main residence was in Hertfordshire but he may have lived at Hornerthorpe when visiting the brickworks. The Marsh Horner & Co brickworks however became insolvent and in 1867 was the subject of a winding up order and subsequently sold to or taken over by the Portland Cement Co, including the house named Hornerthorpe. From the late

19th and early 20th century Hornerthorpe was also a grocery shop and a beer house.

Hornerthorpe, Butt Lane, Burgh Castle

The small holding comprised of 5 ¼ acres, premises, all fitted with electric light, comprise: brick, stone and tiled barn, store shed, two timber and corrugated iron roofed sheds (one with dog kennel), an excellent modern building 97' x 24'6'' recently constructed of brick with steel trusses, asbestos roof, roof lights, steel framed windows, sliding door and concrete floor, 2,500 gallon soft water storage tank, piggeries, well-built of timber lined and heavy gauge corrugated iron roof and runs with centre passage and deep litter house at end, root-house, large farrowing box, and good timber lined stable.

The Botwrights had a stall on Yarmouth market since the 1880s so Frud had experience of selling produce in this way. Once the market garden was up and running, Frud and Anne established their own stall on Yarmouth market. They grew and sold produce with which they were well familiar from their days at Pansy Villa in Belton, including tomatoes, cucumbers, lettuces, radishes, spring onions, potatoes, turnips, rhubarb and numerous varieties of cut flowers such as asters, dahlias, pinks, chrysanthemums, sweet peas, gladiolas, rodanthemums, calendula, pyrethrums, marguerites, scotch thistles, gypsophila, asters, statice, helichrysum, anemones, stocks and cornflowers, to name but a few.

Fred and Anne gathering strawberries

Frud was 60 when he set up on his own but had
an invaluable life's experience as a market
gardener and in social discourse. He used
humour and innuendo to great effect on the stall.
A few customers expected to be greeted with a
good morning madam or sir, but most were
working class folk who enjoyed a bit of banter.
There is nothing worse than being confronted
with shop or stall staff with a sour faced
expression and deathly serious persona. Frud
utilised his gift to great effect, customers will
come back as long as the product is good, the
price is reasonable and their experience was
enjoyable.

Frud and Anne on their market stall circa 1960.

Frud loved to have the opportunity to 'pull the leg' of customers. A customer moaning about the price of Frud's Victoria plums, stating they are much cheaper on another stall, *yes missus*, he said, *but have you seen the size of my plums*! A lady asked for two tomatoes, as opposed to the usual request for a 1lb, his retort, *having company*? Oh your radishes look lovely said a lady, Frud said, *they eat really well but they do make me rise (fart) so*! Growing cucumbers was a difficult and skilful task, preparing the bed and stringing the plants up on wires to ensure that a nice long and straight cucumber was achieved. Invariably some cucumbers did not grow straight despite his best efforts, being curly yet still perfectly edible and a loss of earnings if thrown away. Frud's answer was to advocate the value and special flavour of 'carly cues'.

One customer had a speech impediment, she replaced the sound of the letters t k c and g with the sound of the letter d. So "a pound of tomatoes and a cucumber" would sound like "a pound of domadoes and a dudumber". Frud was a good mimic and could perfectly represent her speech. When she came to the stall Frud would make himself busy so Anne had to serve her, he would then stand behind Anne doing a quiet vocal impression of the customer making Anne laugh much to her annoyance. From then on Anne busied herself when the customer came to the stall, forcing Frud to serve her, as she knew she couldn't help but laugh at the customer's speech, although not in an unkind way.

In the middle of a very hot and busy summer period on the stall, Frud got one of the lads from the village to work on the stall to help out. The lad wore some very short and baggy shorts, poor Anne noticed that every time the lad crouched down to pick up a box of veg to restock the stall something was hanging out of the leg of his shorts, that is to say not one thing but two things. Anne, not wishing to embarrass the lad, mentioned this to Frud, who had no compunction in saying out loud to the lad *"my missus tells me your gotta good pair o'plums there"*. To which Anne tutted and said you might as well have broadcast that to the whole market.

Frud was also artful on the stall, purposefully misspelling words or pricing something as if in error, such as disbudded chrysanthemums 6 for 1/- or 12 for 2/-. Many customers stopped to point out these errors but in the process then purchased something from the stall!

Frud began to grow succulents which he thought would sell on the stall, one of which was an Aeonium. The mischievous Frud wrote the label for the plant name so customers would know what it was, and on the label he wrote 'Giant Arsoleum', the customers assuming it was a Latin plant name to which they were unfamiliar.

Frud and Anne had to get up at 4am on Market Day and they wouldn't get home until 6pm, a very long and tiresome day for them. They therefore always went to bed after Sunday Lunch to catch up on their sleep. The trouble was that Frud had a habit of snoring, keeping Anne awake, a dig in the ribs usually worked but occasionally Anne would have to shout "stop snoring" to which Frud responded *"snowing be buggered"*.

Despite the loss of the railway in 1959 which served Belton and Burgh Castle, Frud continued to send cut flowers away by train. British Rail, as it was then known, collected bulky items by lorry and delivered them to the nearest station. These Scammell Scarab articulated trucks were really unusual as they had a 3-wheeled tractor unit.

British Rail Scammell Scarab truck
Supermac1961 from CHAFFORD HUNDRED, England
(https://commons.wikimedia.org/wiki/File:Scammell_3_wheeler_truck_-_Flickr_-
_Supermac1961.jpg), „Scammell 3 wheeler truck - Flickr - Supermac1961",
https://creativecommons.org/licenses/by/2.0/legalcode

Frud and Anne made a reasonable living on their smallholding, they also had instant access to fresh vegetables, they kept chickens for eggs and meat, and their son Derek kept and bred pigs mostly Large White, Large Black and Saddleback. Crushed oyster shell was fed to the chickens to alleviate soft eggshells and a china egg was placed in the nest box to encourage the chickens to lay.

Frud liked a drink and would frequently play jokes on the pub customers and staff. On one occasion, he broke a tiny piece off a Swan Vesta match and placed it in his ear, he then told his fellow drinkers how wonderful his new hearing aid was, hearing aids at this time were large and cumbersome and the people could not believe this tiny 'match end' was actually a hearing aid, it even got to the stage where people were standing behind him and saying in a quiet voice "can you hear me now" yes said Frud. The irony was that Frud by now did indeed have a hearing aid, a big boxy thing which lived in his breast pocket and connected by a wire to his ear piece which completely filled his ear and was not unnoticeable. His hearing aid was forever emitting a piercing shrill whistle which Frud could not hear but which annoyed everyone else around him immensely.

He had a small box on the back of his bike and he convinced the landlady of the Tavern that he had a 'water otter' in this box, she was appalled and very concerned for the animal's welfare, "that'll die in there in this heat, how long has it been in there, has it had a drink" she insisted on taking some water out to the 'water otter', only to find when Frud lifted the lid of the box a kettle therein. Some of the patrons didn't take kindly to Frud making them look daft and some got their revenge by urinating into his car's petrol tank, causing the car to breakdown on the way home.

Frud's daughter Marjorie was a frequent visitor, she was very close to her mother Anne. Marjorie complained about a problem with her arm, being unable to raise it higher than her shoulder. So off went Marjorie and Anne to the doctor, having explained the problem, the doctor said well how high were you able to raise your arm, to which she replied, well right up here, demonstrating as if a pupil in class putting their hand up to be excused.

Marjorie also got in to her mother's bad books. Anne made her a cup of coffee, when Marjorie started to drink this she exclaimed have you changed your brand of coffee, this tastes strange. To which, highly annoyed at the criticism and becoming obstropolous (obstreperous) Anne said what's wrong with my coffee, you've had it before, but once tasted she had to concede it did taste peculiar. Gravy salt, at this time, came in cardboard packets and it had a propensity to go hard, to resolve this Anne would empty the cardboard packet of gravy salt into an empty coffee jar and obviously had chosen the wrong jar when making the coffee on this occasion.

Something which made Anne annoyed was when Frud was given a cup of hot tea, he wouldn't wait for it to cool, instead, he would pour the tea into his saucer, blow on it to cool it and then loudly slurp the tea. Anne's response, "oh for goodness sake Freddums, do you have to?" in a very scolding manner.

1965 to 1972 Roman Way

At the age of 72, Frud decided that he would retire, he put Hornerthorpe up for sale and had a bungalow built on part of the land for him and Anne to live out their remaining years. The bungalow was appropriately named Roman Way, as the near 2000 year old Roman Fort at Burgh Castle could be viewed from his front room window.

Frud and Anne outside 'Roman Way'

Frud had purchased a Ford Anglia 100E from the wife of the buyer of Hornerthorpe. It was a pig to start, especially on cold damp mornings and this was exacerbated by the new asbestos garage that Frud had built. The damp penetrated the HT leads which ran from the distributor to the plugs. Many a time did Frud require a tow to get it started, much to the peril of the tower! His oldest grandson appeared on the scene on one of these occasions, give us a tow said Frud. Grandson tied a rope to the back of his car and the front of Frud's Ford Anglia, off down the road they went. The usual protocol when towing is for the towee to sound his horn or flash his lights once the car had started, the tower would then stop, untie the rope and both cars would depart on their journeys. It appears as though Frud was unfamiliar with this procedure, his car quickly started, unbeknown to grandson, but grandson soon knew that it had started when he saw Frud overtaking him with said tow rope still attached!

Frud never passed a driving test as there was no such thing when he began to drive and for the rest of his life he really did not master the art of driving. For some unknown reason, his wide-brimmed trilby, usually worn on the horizontal, was worn on the back of his head 45° off horizontal when he was driving. Before the use of traffic lights policemen would stand on a raised platform at busy junctions directing traffic and keeping the traffic flowing freely, a dangerous task in the middle of a busy crossroads especially if a car wanted to make a right turn, one of Frud's attempts at this manoeuvre resulted in the policeman being knocked off his platform. Another advancement relating to the motor car and to ease congestion on roads originally designed for a horse and cart was the one-way system. Frud was either not aware of this introduction in Great Yarmouth or choose to ignore it. Regent road became one-way, but Frud was completely oblivious to this and the huge No Entry sign, making his journey to the market via the same route he had used for years, only to be stopped by a policeman. Frud had this incredible gift to placate people and talk his way out of anything, this he did by calling the policeman 'sergeant' when he was only a constable and stating "well I've driven up here for years, well how long has it been one-way" he was let off with a 'don't do it again'.

Frud's son Derek, accompanied by his wife and son would frequently take Frud and Anne out 'for a ride' on a Sunday afternoon around the neighbouring villages of Belton, Lound, Somerleyton and Ashby, hardly foreign climes but people were easily satisfied at this time and the scenery around the Somerleyton estate is wonderful, especially in June when the rhododendrons are in bloom. One of Frud's comedic and favourite expressions when espying some unusual feature or scenic cottage or view was '*look, look Anne, you may never pass this way again*'. On one occasion the car boiled over and emptied the radiator in a place called Ashby Dell, the car had broken down in the Dell with a hill in front and behind, so unable to push the car. A visit to the nearest house for a jug of water to refill the radiator resolved the dilemma. Another occasion saw the engine cough and splutter when driving up hill, regaining power when levelling out, this continued until they got home. The removal of the petrol tank and subsequent emptying thereof revealed a piece of cloth which had been covering the petrol outlet when the car was inclined.

*Frud and Anne at How Hill, Ludham, with son
Derek and grandson Kenny*

Frud could talk to anyone and was also
extremely tactile, he had to touch the person he
was talking to. A trip to the Somerleyton Dukes
Head perfectly demonstrated this fact. Frud,
Anne, his son, daughter in law and grandson
were sitting at a table in the pub, on the next
table were a young courting couple, obviously
head over heels in love and wishing to whisper
sweet nothings in each other's ear. Frud moves

his chair, very slightly towards the couple's table, and then a little bit closer, and a bit closer still, until he was no longer seated on the family's table but on the table of the courting couple, in deep conversation with them and with his hand on the young girl's knee, Frud was an extremely tactile person, seemingly unable to talk to anyone, male or female, without laying his hand upon their person, almost as if preventing them from getting away.

Frud's youngest grandson spent time during school holidays at his grandparents newly built bungalow, helping with gardening and cutting the lawn whilst his parents were at work. Frud had lots of tools and equipment from his market garden including a wooden barrow made by his brother-in-law Henry. Grandson was sat on one of the barrow's shafts and Frud decided he too would sit in this location, all was well until a loud creaking sound which was the precursor of the shaft breaking and Frud and grandson went base over apex. Grandson also innocently picked up a book which was lying beside Frud's chair in the front room and began reading, Anne was unperturbed by this, thinking it's good for a young child to read, when Frud came in the room, noticed what grandson was reading, instantly snatching it from his grasp and stormed out muttering to himself. The book was, The Perfumed Garden, which gives advice on sexual technique, warnings about sexual health, and recipes to remedy sexual maladies, not appropriate reading for a 12 year old grandson.

Frud decided he needed some canes for his plants, so on a visit to his son Peter's market garden in Browston he decided to help himself, it would have been simpler to just ask his son for some canes but Frud decided he would snaffle some concealing them across his shoulders within his jacket. These 'stood out like a sore thumb' and Peter and his family assumed that Frud had put his jacket on with the coat hanger still inside!

Frud enjoyed his weekly visit to his son Peter's market garden followed by a pint or two or three on the way home. The visits were nearly always eventful, on one occasion he stood staring out of the window exclaiming "that is a wonderful view" when smoke started bellowing from his pocket as a result of his lit pipe, requiring him to be 'put out' by a jug of water. Having always lived in the country when Frud wanted a wee he just had one, wherever he was, usually in a field or against a hedge, but this liberal approach to urination was also undertaken in Peter's front garden, much to the annoyance of the neighbours.

Peter's market garden at 'Crossways' Browston, was owned by the Knights family in the early part of the 20th century. Mr Knights was a very solemn and sombre man who had lost his wife. His children had little to eat and their clothes induced people to consider them ragamuffins. His son William (Billy) Herbert Knights frequently visited Pansy Villa where Frud's wife Anne provided him with food, a fact that Billy never forgot, as evidenced by his outpouring of emotion at Anne's funeral. Billy left Browston in 1928, married Florence and set up a small business rearing cows at West Bilney. He had no money, so he audaciously contacted a farmer, admitting he had no funds and offering a proposal to take some cows from the farmer, fatten them and pay for them when he sold them.

The farmer appreciated Billy's dilemma and admired his tenacity and agreed. Billy and Florence lived frugally, saving the profits from the sale of the cows and eventually bought a smallholding at Gooderstone. By this time Billy and Florence had three sons and a daughter. W. H. Knights & Sons began growing carrots and parsnips, suited to the sandy soil of the Brecks, supplying the supermarkets. The business grew considerably, he rented more land and eventually farmed over 2000 acres, adding salad crops such as iceberg lettuce and spring onions for the supermarkets. He also had a huge factory where the carrots were delivered by tractor and trailer, tipped into a hopper and into the factory by conveyor. The carrots were washed, graded and packed coming out the other end of the factory into articulated trucks and delivered around the country. Billy invited Frud and Anne to Gooderstone, to stay in his newly built bungalow. Frud whose experience of agriculture was a horse and cart plus an antiquated tractor, marvelled at the size of Billy's operation, the automated factory, the huge modern four wheeled drive tractors and trucks. Everything Billy shew him produced *"Cuh, look Anne, look, well wadaya think o'that"*. Billy had an accident as a young man when he was trapped underneath a tractor causing him significant injuries from which he never fully recovered, for this reason he purchased a Citroen DS Pallas, due to the fact that it had 'air suspension' and, at the press of a button, it could be raised up six inches to provide ground clearance to negotiate furrows when travelling around the fields. Billy did this daily to inspect the crops and in readiness for the daily family breakfast meeting. The technology of Billy's car was met with *"well I never, Anne look at that, he just presses a button and the car raise up, well wadaya think o'that"*. Frud was equally flabbergasted, astonished and overwhelmed when Billy's son took him up in his light aircraft from his own airstrip. This wasn't the first time Frud had been in an aircraft as an animal feedstuff supplier 'Press, Bly & Davey' took him for a flight over Belton as a thank you for his custom.

A night club owner from London moved into Burgh Castle and invited some of the male villagers to his house including Frud. What they didn't know was that some young ladies would be in attendance and whose club role was that of 'bunny girls' they wore a costume called a "bunny suit" inspired by the tuxedo-wearing Playboy rabbit mascot, consisting of a strapless corset teddy, bunny ears, black pantyhose, a bow tie, a collar, cuffs and a fluffy cottontail.. Somehow Anne suspected or got to know about these young ladies and went to the house to fetch Frud home, his response being *"Well Anne, wadaya think o'that, I'm suffin glad you rescued me as I think that them young girls were about to molest me!"*

Frud died at Roman Way, Burgh Castle, the village of his birth, at the age of 80. Frud would have been astounded and dismayed at the wholesale development of his beloved village of Belton, the demise of the horticultural industry, the loss of the fields once filled with glass houses and flowers, he would definitely have said to Anne *'well wadaya think o'that'*.

Bunny Girls

Christiano Oliveira
(https://commons.wikimedia.org/wiki/File:Brazilian_playmates_at_Campus_Party_Br
asil_2009_ (2).jpg), „Brazilian playmates at Campus Party Brasil 2009 (2)",
https://creativecommons.org/licenses/by/2.0/legalcode

Lothingland

Mutford and Lothingland was a Hundred of
Suffolk, with an area of 33,368 acres, including
Lowestoft, the most easterly point of Great
Britain. Mutford and Lothingland Hundred
formed the north-eastern corner of Suffolk.
Around five miles wide, but fifteen miles from
north to south it was bounded by Norfolk to the
north and west, and the North Sea to the east,
other than the strip of land occupied by Great
Yarmouth, Norfolk. Little Yarmouth
(Southtown) and Gorleston-on-Sea were to the
west of the River Yare and geographically within
Suffolk. The Hundred's border with Norfolk
was formed by the River Waveney as it bends
north on its final approaches to the sea, Breydon
Water and the River Yare. It was separated to
the south from the Hundreds of Wangford and
Blything by the appropriately named Hundred
River.

Mutford and Lothingland Incorporation:-Ashby,
Barnby, Belton, Blundeston, Bradwell, Burgh
Castle, Carlton Colville, Corton, Flixton, Fritton
Gisleham, Gorleston-with Southtown (Little
Yarmouth), Gunton, Herringfleet, Hopton,

Kessingland, Kirkley, Lound, Lowestoft, Mutford, Oulton, Pakefield, Rushmere, Somerleyton.

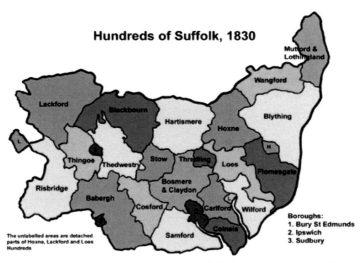

Hundreds of Suffolk, 1830

Smb1001 (https://commons.wikimedia.org/wiki/File:Suffolk_Hundreds_1830.png), „Suffolk Hundreds 1830", https://creativecommons.org/licenses/by-sa/3.0/legalcode

Post 1974, the administration of five parishes in the northern most tip of Suffolk were taken over by Norfolk due to boundary changes. Belton with Browston, Bradwell, Burgh Castle, Hopton, Fritton and St Olaves were all Suffolk communities, one third of the settlements in Lothingland Half-Hundred, a very ancient administrative district dating back to the Anglo-

Saxon period. There is evidence of human activity in this area going back to the Palaeolithic Period (Old Stone Age).

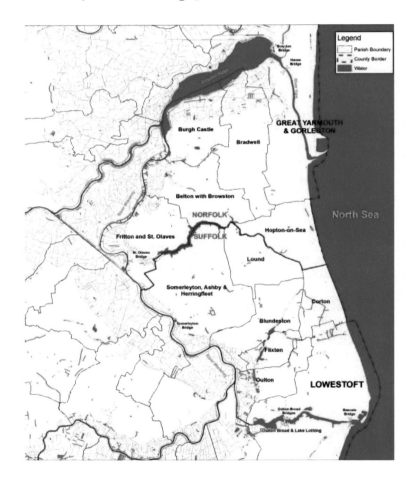

Lothingland is essentially an island, with the River Yare and the North Sea to the East, Breydon Water (the remnants of a huge tidal estuary) to the North, the River Waveney to its West, and Oulton Dyke and Oulton Broad to the South.

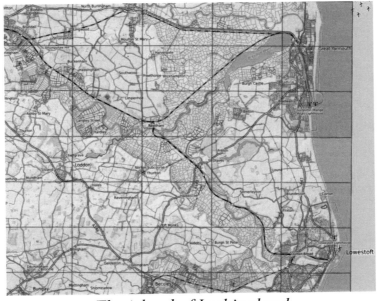

The island of Lothingland

Places of Interest in Lothingland

Lothingland has many places of interest including the impressive and well preserved, near 2000 year old, Roman fort (Garianonum) at Burgh Castle, two 19th century brick works, one at Burgh Castle and one at Somerleyton, numerous WWII pill boxes and anti-tank defences, wind pumps and windmills, including an octagonal three-storey smock mill at Herringfleet, the 13th century Augustinian St Olaves Priory, numerous Round Tower Churches, the wonderful Somerleyton estate, Hall and Gardens, two sites where duck decoy traps were installed and used, one at Fritton and one at Flixton, the rivers Yare, Waveney and Oulton Broad, integral components of the Norfolk Broads and also the seaside.

Belton Common was used by the military in WW1 and WW2. It contained numerous trenches for training purposes, guns and a searchlight.

BELTON COMMON WW2
(Not to accurate scale)

▬▬▬▬ WW2 Trenches
●━●━●━● Pre WW2 Trenches

With kind permission of Dick Lindsay – Belton/Burgh Castle Mardle, Norfolk

Fritton Lake is nearly 3 miles long and covers an area of 170 acres surrounded by woodland. In the middle of the 19th century there were eight decoy pipes in use and thirteen disused pipes still visible, making twenty one in all. Several villages border the Lake including Fritton, St Olaves, Herringfleet, Ashby, Lound, Belton and

Browston. Colonel Leathes of Herringfleet Hall worked three pipes and stated that these have been worked by his family for 160 years and is certain that they existed for over 200 years. Decoy pipes have therefore been in existence on the Lake since 1650 and probably before that. In the latter part of the 19th century, up to 4000 ducks were taken each season, from November to March, using the decoy pipes. The word decoy derives from Holland, where decoys originated. It is an abbreviation of 'endekooy' i.e. the 'duck cage' used to describe the tunnels of net resembling cages or pipes. In 17th century decoys the ducks were enticed into the tunnel-like structure with food, latter decoy pipes used boats, and dogs, appearing and disappearing behind reed screens, to drive the ducks into the trap. There is evidence that the trapping of ducks existed in a similar but maybe not as efficient form in the 13th century.

A decoy comprised of narrowing netted hooped tunnels called pipes. The number of tunnels could be from three to eight in a decoy. Numerous tunnels were required so as to suit the wind direction, as ducks swim and fly into the wind. Therefore a pipe had to be selected that the wind is blowing out of, to accommodate the direction they swim and fly. If the wind is blowing into the entrance to the pipe the ducks will turn and head out of the pipe when rising. A three to five pipe decoy was considered optimal.

The pipes are the long, curving, net-covered ditches into which the ducks are driven and captured. The first hoop of the pipe is usually 20 feet wide tapering off at the end of the 60 metre ditch to 2 feet wide. The height of the pipe at the entrance is 12 to 15 feet high falling to 2 feet high at the end of the pipe wherein the ducks are caught. Along the side of the first two thirds of the pipe are placed 12 foot long and 6 foot wide reed screens. A dog weaves in and out of these screens to drive them up the pipe. The diagram shows a piece of open water from one to three acres with five pipes leading off it.

PLAN OF DECOY WITH 5 PIPES,

SCALE—120 FT TO AN INCH.

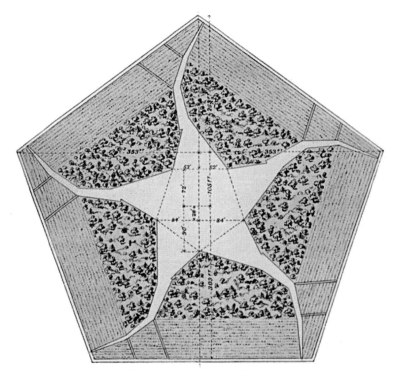

Sir Ralph Frankland-Payne-Gallwey, 3rd Baronet (1848-1916)
(https://commons.wikimedia.org/wiki/File:Decoy_5_pipe.png), „Decoy 5 pipe",
marked as public domain, more details on Wikimedia Commons:
https://commons.wikimedia.org/wiki/Template:PD-old

*The three previous images show the entrance,
interior and the end of a decoy pipe.*
Norfolk Broads and Rivers (1884) G. C. Davies

*Sir Ralph Frankland-Payne-Gallwey, 3rd Baronet (1848-1916)
(https://commons.wikimedia.org/wiki/File:Decoy_in_action.png), „Decoy in action",
marked as public domain, more details on Wikimedia Commons:
https://commons.wikimedia.org/wiki/Template:PD-old*

229

Boarstall Duck Decoy

Fritton Lake

Jennings, Payne (1843 - 1926)
http://ogimages.bl.uk/images/006/006ZZZ10360AA25U00011000[SVC1].jpg

Fritton Lake

Evelyn Simak
(https://commons.wikimedia.org/wiki/File:View_across_Fritton_Decoy_-
geograph.org.uk-_806141.jpg), „View across Fritton Decoy - geograph.org.uk -
806141", https://creativecommons.org/licenses/by-sa/2.0/legalcode

Frozen Fritton Lake

Pete Chapman
(https://commons.wikimedia.org/wiki/File:Frozen_Fritton_Decoy,_Herringfleet,_Nea
r_Lowestoft,_Suffolk_-_geograph.org.uk_-_30105.jpg), „Frozen Fritton Decoy,
Herringfleet, Near Lowestoft, Suffolk - geograph.org.uk - 30105",
https://creativecommons.org/licenses/by-sa/2.0/legalcode

During both WWI and WWII, Lothingland contained numerous training and defensive sites. Aerial photography shows a group of World War One and World War Two practice trenches on Belton Common. Fritton Lake may have been a WW1 Royal Naval Air Service seaplane base. In 1940 wire hawsers were fixed across the lake at 70 yard intervals to prevent German seaplanes from landing. Two P 47 Thunderbolts collided above the lake during World War Two. The lake was used for testing the amphibious tanks used in the D-Day Normandy Landings. There were anti-aircraft guns at Belton Common and Herringfleet, a WWI airfield at Burgh Castle and a massive underground WWII Ground-Controlled Interception (GCI) Radar Station at RAF Hopton.

WW1 Royal Naval Air Service reconnaissance,
bombing and torpedo-carrying seaplane

DD Sherman amphibious tank with its flotation screen lowered.

DD or Duplex Drive tank, functioned by erecting a 'flotation screen' around the tank, which enabled it to float, and it had two propellers powered by the tank's engine to drive them in the water. Valentine DDs were used for training and the majority of the US, British, and Canadian DD crews did their preliminary training with them. Crews learned elementary phases of the DD equipment at Fritton Lake, on the

Norfolk/Suffolk border. Here they learnt to waterproof and maintain their tanks, use Amphibious Tank Escape Apparatus, launch from mock up LCT ramps and navigate around the two and a half mile lake.

In 1993 a Catalina flying boat landed on Fritton Lake, much to everyone's excitement.

PBY Catalina
amphibious aircraft or flying boat
anonymous (https://commons.wikimedia.org/wiki/File:PBY_Catalina_landing.jpg),
„PBY Catalina landing", marked as public domain, more details on Wikimedia
Commons: https://commons.wikimedia.org/wiki/Template:PD-US

Gariannonum, the Roman Fort at Burgh Castle

The Roman Stablesian Cavalry based at Garianonum used boats to get about and moored these in a safe haven, currently known as Stepshort, a location that straddles the Main Dyke that forms the border between Belton and Burgh Castle. The following map shows how much bigger this was at this time. Boats were used out of necessity as the surrounding land was mostly flooded at high tide and mud flats at low tide, not conducive to land based travel. Boats were also much quicker to get troops to a location where marauding Saxon and Frank seaborne invaders were raiding the coastline as the area at this time was more water than land. The Roman Forts at Burgh Castle and Caister were strategically located at the south and north of a large estuary, and the confluence of many rivers which were a gateway to inland settlements, ideal for the seaborne invaders.

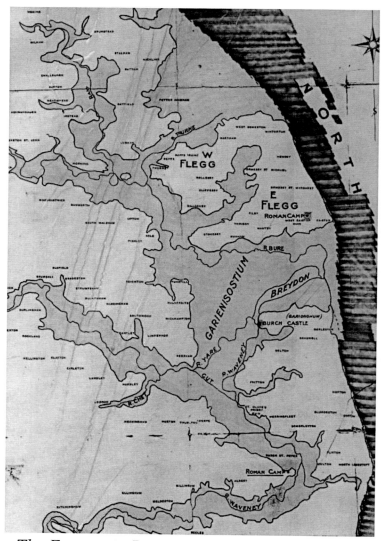

*The Estuary in Roman Times, Great Yarmouth
did not exist then.*

Belton

There is evidence of human activity in Belton dating to the Palaeolithic or Old Stone Age period. Belton, Beletun or Bolton, as it has been recorded, has the suffix 'ton' denoting a Saxon homestead / farmhouse, 'bel' can mean dry ground / island and the village is surrounded on three sides by water. General consensus has the development i.e. permanent dwellings, of Belton originating around The Green, adjacent to a small stream providing fresh water, with roads leading from this area to Fritton and Bradwell. The Green may have been the village green or common grazing land, the location of a market and adjacent to the 17th century Tithe Barn, which may well have earlier origins. Locklees Lane (now Station Road North and South) may not have been a permanent road until the erection of the river wall. The name Locklees Lane was still in use in 1886, 30 years after the railway came to Belton. Lock in Old English can mean barrier and Lees in Old English can mean sediment, concluding a sedimentary barrier, probably the extent to which the water reached when the marshes to the west flooded prior to the construction of a river wall. Similarly, St Johns Road bordered the estuary shoreline but the road name possibly derives from 'The manor of Caxton Hall formerly appertained to the prior and knights of St John of Jerusalem, and Gapton Hall, a portion of which lies in the Parish, belonging to the Priory of Leigh, in Essex which was dedicated to St John the Evangelist and owned by Gapton Hall Manor'.

Map of the main populated part of Belton 1884
'Reproduced with the permission of the National Library of Scotland (CC BY 4.0)'

The land to the North and East of Locklees Lane, which gradually rises, may therefore have been free from flooding and hence why this area was settled. Indeed Belton in the last millennia would have been tantamount to a peninsular surrounded on three sides by the flood plains of the River Waveney to the West, the Main Dyke to the North and another dyke to the South, both of these dykes being much wider and navigable. Today these flood plains are marshland, fenland or wooded carrs, mainly due to the construction of the river wall and drainage pumps, currently motor powered, but prior to the 20th century, wind powered drainage mills.

The 25 ft contour projects into Belton from the East, the surrounding land falling away to 0 ft.

The Parish is that of 'Belton with Browston'. The former classified as a Village and the latter a Hamlet and separated by the A143, a former toll road, with the crossroads known colloquially as the turnpike i.e. one of the places where the toll to use the road was collected and used to maintain the road. Road maintenance was taken over in the late 19th century by the Rural District and then County Councils. Prior to this the Parish Surveyor of Highways was responsible for road repairs, acquiring appropriate material from pits around the parish of which there were four. Roads at this time were not tar and stone, they were literally dirt tracks, compacted by use. The tar and stone surfacing of the parish roads occurred gradually during the 1920s.

John Druery in his 1826 book describes turning off the turnpike road into Belton as such *'pursuing this road for nearly a mile, a low sequestered dell, having a few houses, denotes the entrance to Belton'*. The fact that entering Belton with its west facing slope means that the village is unseen until actually within it, is still the case, the only exception now being the houses on Church Lane can be seen, but of course these were not there at this time and Belton largely remains hidden from view.

In a 1900 listing of Belton it states, soil is a light land; subsoil, sand. The chief crops are barley, turnips, wheat and hay. The area is 2,030 acres, 674 of which, on the river side, are marsh land, 27 of water and 9 of tidal water; the population in 1891 was 752.

Belton 1906

The maps above and following shows the gradual increase of dwellings from 1906 to 1928, with the main development during this period occurring on Station Road North, yet the population remained fairly static at around 830 souls from 1900 right up to 1960.

Belton 1928

The population of Belton for hundreds of years was between three and four hundred souls increasing to 800+ during the late 19th and early 20th centuries. The population of Belton ballooned to 4000 with development in the village in the late 1960s and early 1970s. The following two images illustrate, via a map dated

1950, how few houses there were in Belton at this time, and, via an aerial image taken in 2020, how Belton has developed and grown. The majority of the large buildings seen on the 1950s map are glass houses relating to the numerous market gardens as opposed to dwellings.

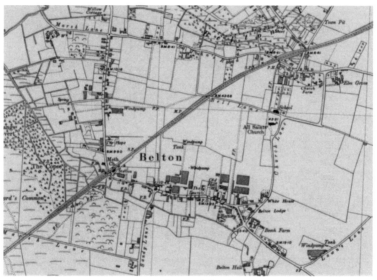

Belton 1950

The following page:

Belton 2020

Image supplied by Peter Roll

Bibliography

Auxiliary Units
https://en.wikipedia.org/wiki/Auxiliary_Units

Baedeker Blitz
https://en.wikipedia.org/wiki/Baedeker_Blitz

Belton History
http://beals.info/genealogy/sources/belton_history.htm

Boatwright / Boatright Family Genealogy
http://www.boatwrightgenealogy.com/index.html

Charabanc
https://en.wikipedia.org/wiki/Charabanc

Dazzle camouflage
https://en.wikipedia.org/wiki/Dazzle_camouflage

DD Tank
https://en.wikipedia.org/wiki/DD_tank

Historical and topographical Notices of Great Yarmouth in Norfolk and its Environs, including the Parishes and Hamlets of the Half Hundred of Lothingland in Suffolk (1826) John Henry Druery

Market Garden
https://en.wikipedia.org/wiki/Market_garden CC BY-SA

Military Service Act 1916
https://en.wikipedia.org/wiki/Military_Service_Act_1916

Motor Launch
https://en.wikipedia.org/wiki/Motor_Launch

Norfolk Broads and Rivers (1884) G. C. Davies

Norwich Blitz
https://en.wikipedia.org/wiki/Norwich_Blitz

Shooting-brake
https://en.wikipedia.org/wiki/Shooting-brake

St Nazaire Raid
https://en.wikipedia.org/wiki/St_Nazaire_Raid

Suffolk Punch
https://en.wikipedia.org/wiki/Suffolk_Punch

Sun pictures of the Norfolk Broads: one hundred photographs from nature of the rivers and broads of Norfolk and Suffolk (1891) by Payne Jennings.

The Book of Duck Decoys: Their Construction, Management and History (1886) Ralph Payne-Gallwey.

The Roman Camp and the Irish Saint at Burgh Castle (1913) Louis H. Dahl

Yarmouth–Beccles line
https://en.wikipedia.org/wiki/Yarmouth%E2%80%93Beccles_line